THE INTUITION PRINCIPLE

HOW TO ATTRACT THE LIFE YOU DREAM OF

ANGELA ARTEMIS

Formatted by Launchpad Press, Cody, WY
www.launchpad-press.com

ISBN : 978-0-9837-454-0-2

Library of Congress Control Number: 2011934834

First Edition, January 2012
Printed in the United States of America

Praise for *The Intuition Principle*

"I know that everyone has experienced that sinking feeling when something goes very wrong and you say to yourself, 'I knew it. Something told me not to listen to that advice. I should have just followed my gut.' *The Intuition Principle* addresses this and so much more. It is a blueprint for how to tap into your intuition, listen to your 'gut' and pursue your true goals. It also teaches you how to identify those goals and overcome your fears so you can live your dreams. Whether you know what you want or are deciding your direction, the book will give you tools you need to go after and attain your dreams. Everyone should read it."

— Rosemarie Monaco, President, Group M Inc., *www.GroupM.org*

"We all have an inner GPS to guide us towards clarity when we are lost in a fog of indecision and overwhelm. The trouble is, most of us have no clue how to use it. I felt like Angela was right beside me, teaching me how to activate and strengthen my intuition. I now honor voices and nudges that point me towards paths I previously would have turned away from, and my life is healthier and happier as a result."

— Jean Berg-Sarauer

"Angela's book, *The Intuition Principle*, can really change your life—no matter what your walk in life is. With her examples and encouragement, intuition can become a guiding force on your pathway to happiness, success, and self-discovery. Her sincerity, belief, and hope for her readers to find a better life come across on every page. I highly recommend keeping a copy by your bedside or desktop to refer to Angela's wisdom and learn about your own inner wisdom."

— Janet Dengel

How to get the most from this book

There are numerous exercises in the book that will help you become familiar with and develop your intuition. Each chapter is designed to build your knowledge and skill set for working with your intuition; this will make it easier for you to discover your passion and true calling in later chapters. The best way to go through the book is by reading each chapter and completing all the exercises in the order in which they are presented. You will find your intuitive abilities increase easily and naturally if you follow this sequence.

Contents

"How do geese know when to fly to the sun? Who tells them the seasons? How do we, humans, know when it is time to move on? How do we know when to go? As with the migrant birds, so surely with us, there is a voice within, if only we would listen to it, that tells us so certainly when to go forth into the unknown."

—Elisabeth Kubler-Ross, M.D.

Introduction
The Intuition Principle

"The intuitive mind is a sacred gift and the rational mind is a faithful servant. We have created a society that honors the servant and has forgotten the gift."
— Albert Einstein

When you live an intuitively inspired life the world will come to you

Does exerting less effort to accomplish your goals appeal to you?

Are you tired of over-thinking everything and still feeling unsure about making the right choice?

If you answered yes to either of these questions then you might want to think about developing your intuition and psychic abilities, also known as extrasensory perception or the sixth sense.

When I was younger I wasn't in touch with my intuition. I was afraid to trust it and follow my dreams of becoming a writer. I came to write this book because not being in touch with my intuition ultimately stifled my growth and happiness. I felt called to share with others the lessons I learned in my search to reconnect to my intuition. I hoped my experience might save others from going through what I had; I wasted so much time pursuing the wrong path.

You wouldn't know it from your everyday life, but you are much more extraordinary than you think you are. Your consciousness exists on many more levels than you are aware of and has access to an infinite realm of intelligence at all times. When you access this Greater Intelligence[1] and infinite source of creativity, you become better at solving problems and making decisions, which contributes to your success in life. Developing and using your intuition is a very practical skill to have.

Intuition, which includes psychic ability, opens up a wider range of thought processes. You are able to tap into what Swiss psychologist Carl Jung[2] called the "collective unconscious,"[3] and what I refer to as Greater Intelligence. Jung's "collective unconscious" presupposed that humanity had access to a vast storehouse of universal knowledge. This field of greater intelligence is the source of true knowledge. When you tap into the collective unconscious you will spontaneously begin to receive answers to questions that have been plaguing you for a very long time.

Learning to use your extrasensory perception expands your mind by connecting you with your true creative nature and your infinite potential. It doesn't take all that long to hone your abilities and learn how to tap into your intuition either. Learning to use this natural ability is effortless and fun.

Most people never fully utilize their extrasensory perception. Our culture doesn't value this way of acquiring knowledge. We were sent to schools and told to memorize facts and mathematical formulas. All that mattered was quantifiable knowledge. Intuition, though, is an innate intelligence that everyone is born with. Once you begin to develop it you will see how quickly it all comes back to you—not unlike riding a bike. You never forget.

Living authentically

When you are in touch with your intuition you are also in touch with your authenticity. The authentic you is the pure and unbridled potential

1   Authors note: I use the term Greater Intelligence in place of "creator" or God.

2   Funk&Wagnalls New World Encyclopedia Online, s.v. "Jung, Carl Gustav."

3   "Collective unconscious," accessed July 23, 2011, EBSCO*host.*

deep inside of you which, like the acorn, has the potential to become a mighty oak if tended with care. Your authentic self is who you are meant to be. It is who you can become if you trust and allow this potential to manifest. You have to dig deep to reconnect to the authentic you. But first you must learn to trust and follow your intuition.

Your intuition is like your own personal inner guidance system. It will guide you to where you are supposed to go in this life if you let it. When you are connected to your intuition you are joyous. Your life flows. You cannot be swayed by others or conventional wisdom, following them just for the sake of following. You become the leader in your own life, the authentic you who is truly connected to your divine mission and true purpose.

You are here at this time for a purpose. You have a mission in this life and, by reconnecting to your intuition, it will become clear. It will enable you to fulfill your destiny. Your intuition is the voice of your own guidance that will help you find your mission and true purpose.

You will gain insights into why you have had difficulties up until now. And you will understand why certain people are in your life. You will see that even difficult relationships have their place by teaching you life lessons. Your life will finally make sense, and you will understand the broader meaning behind all that you have gone through. All the false layers you have been hiding under will finally fall away, and you will find your true self —the brilliant self you were meant to be.

Your authentic self cannot be maintained unless you establish your connection to Greater Intelligence, which speaks to you through your intuition. To ignore the voice of your intuition is to be disconnected from your source. If you allow others to influence you, undermine you, or if you start to second guess yourself, you begin to sever this delicate new connection. When you start to listen to other people over your intuition, you get mixed up and tripped up. You begin to flounder and no longer feel connected to that inner fire, zeal, and zest for living. You are on your own and under your own very exhaustible steam, cut off from the benefits of this magnificent source.

The secret to having a life that flows is to be guided by this intelligence. When you follow your intuition you have access to an infinite supply of wisdom, creativity, and love. This infinite source will never run out. But you, the human being, can run out of power and find yourself tired and burned out. You can get depressed, down, scared, lost, mixed up, or lose enthusiasm for what you are doing. When Greater Intelligence fuels your efforts, you never encounter any of these problems because you have tapped into the infinite power that created you—the power that knows more than you do.

It takes confidence to be open to this intelligence directing your life. When Greater Intelligence leads the way you follow your intuition and prove that you are strong enough to resign control, no longer basing your decisions on fear. When intuition leads you Greater Intelligence comes in to fill you up. You will never find yourself feeling depleted again—depletion is impossible when you are continually fueled by your intuition. This is the secret to reaching and living your greatness. This intuitive wisdom will inspire you so that you will easily find your way back to the path upon which you were meant to tread.

You have a mission and life plan that contains the unique life lessons you need to learn in order to round out and strengthen your character. You might have to learn how to have harmonious relationships or how to support yourself financially. You may have to learn how to love unconditionally or how to deal with pain and challenges. All those reasons will remain unclear until you learn to tap into your intuition. You have got to be able to hear and trust Greater Intelligence to get back on track and awaken from the dream you have been living. This is when you will start *really* living.

You will never live your authenticity until you partner with your intuition. When you start working with it, instead of shutting it out, a healing will take place in your life. You will no longer allow others to take over your life and control you. You will begin to make wiser choices based on what is right for you—not what is right for anyone else. The people closest to you will sense the changes that have taken place within you immediately. You will allow family members to learn and make their own mistakes without feeling that you have to rush in and save them. You will become a great example to those around you; they will want to listen to their inner guidance as well.

Your self-reliance will stand out and inspire them, as will the resoluteness of your convictions, your confidence, and the strong belief in yourself. As you become who you were meant to be, those around you will learn that they, too, can find and achieve their greatness by emulating you. Your children will learn from you how to be in touch with their authentic selves, and they will pass that it on to their children. This cycle will eventually move throughout the world and become a mainstream principle. When that occurs we will see that it has changed our world for the better.

What is an intuitively inspired life?

To live an intuitively inspired life is to be aligned with your intuitive wisdom. When we are aligned with this wisdom, we naturally gravitate toward those activities that honor our authenticity. Our path and true purpose become clear as we allow intuition to lead us. Conventional thinking no longer sways us; rather, we are moved to share our true talents and gifts with the world in loving service.

Centering our lives upon this wisdom activates a blueprint within us that has been dormant since our birth. This blueprint contains our true potential and reveals the route we are to take to remember what our chosen mission is at this time. As we focus our lives on this mission, and on this guidance, we find the obstacles that held us back in the past begin to fall away. Questions we have had are answered, and all uncertainty we might have experienced about living within this new paradigm disappears.

The journey we take to fulfill our mission reconnects us to our joy and authenticity. We surrender and allow life to flow through us and take us to our next steps easily and effortlessly. We are infused with an energy that streams into us from an inexhaustible source. And, this life force energy carries us over the bumps in the road and headlong to the next steps on our quest. The flow of joy we receive by reconnecting to our authentic selves inspires us to live up to our full potential and greatness; we, in turn, inspire others to reconnect to their intuitive wisdom.

As we live each day, fully connected to our intuitive wisdom, we accomplish more than we could have ever imagined. The journey takes us down roads we never would have imagined we would take. We find ourselves enjoying our lives like never before. We surrender the emotional burdens that had us in knots—those that hindered us from living life fully. As a result we stop worrying so much and become more playful and open to this divine inspiration. By letting go of the need to control everything and moving with this flow we will find that we no longer have to go out and "get" the things in life we desire; rather, they begin to come to us and appear in our lives exactly when they are needed. When we align with our intuition we are resonating with the wisdom that created the Universe and our original purpose. It is this harmony that brings the world to us.

How your intuition brings the world and your dreams to you

"Everything in the universe is within you. Ask all from yourself."
— Rumi

When we learn to go within to look for answers and guidance, we are accessing the source of our very power and of everything that is made manifest in our world. This power runs in, around, and through everything in the entire universe. Without it animating us, our body is nothing more than a lifeless shell.

Greater Intelligence is an organized system whose only directive is the propagation of all life. If what you do supports life on Earth, the Universe is programmed to respond in only one way: by supporting you. When you are on the right path, have found your *raison d'etre*, and use it to help others thrive, you are in-tune with the prime directive of the Universe. Greater Intelligence conspires to help you because your actions support the same goal as the Universe. When you share your gifts and talents in loving service to the world, not only does Greater Intelligence open the way by supporting you, but it also floods your life with true joy, fulfilment, and abundance.

When aligned with this power we also find, or "remember," our true purpose; the world comes to us simply because we are on track according to the blueprint of our lives. The blueprint contains a framework for the experiences we will learn and benefit from. When we are on schedule based on this blueprint the world appears to come to us; it seems as if we are always in the right place at the right time. All that is really happening is that we showed up at the scheduled place of delivery. The point of getting in touch with our intuition is to reconnect to our mission and then begin to show up at the places and events that will actualize our purpose.

Why else would we feel so good about being in certain places and being around certain people we have never met before in this lifetime?

How many times have you met someone and felt as if you had known them throughout your life? When this happens it was meant to happen. You showed up on time in the right place according to the blueprint of your life.

When our lives are full of discord and disharmony it's simply because we are out of alignment with our purpose. We stopped following the blueprint and are now lost. When we go within and allow the Universe to direct our journey, we will find our way and return to the right path. What seem like "miracles" and fortunate and meaningful coincidences will commence.

The secret sauce in life

"Follow your bliss and the universe will open doors where there were only walls."
—Joseph Campbell

Those people who are living their passion and have found their purpose usually lead extraordinary lives. They seem to be blessed, or to have a special aura or energy toward which others gravitate. We watch them in amazement as they accomplish all sorts of marvelous things that we only dream of doing. They have what I call a "fabulousity factor": a direct result of tuning in and living their lives according to the plan they that were meant to follow. They have activated the pure potential within and are living up to that potential fully. They are living their lives "on purpose," and it shows. Everything seems to come so effortlessly to them. When they do encounter "dark clouds," they somehow always find the answers or help they need to come out of it and to find that "silver lining" in all their experiences. You also can have this sensational aspect to your life when you listen to your intuition and get back on the right track in your life by following the path you were meant to follow.

Time for a Pop Quiz!

You are probably much more intuitive than you give yourself credit for.

Take this quiz to see how intuitive you are right now:

1. Do you ever know who is on the phone before you answer it?
2. Do you sometimes get a "knowing" sense about things before they happen?
3. Have you heard talking, or your name being called, just before you fall asleep or wake up?
4. Do you find that you know what people are going to say and can finish their sentences?
5. Have you ever had butterflies in your stomach for no reason and then heard about something happening and they subsided?
6. Are you kind of lucky? Do things have a way of working out for you in your life?
7. During sleep have you experienced being "jarred" or a feeling of falling and landing on the bed?
8. While in the shower or walking in nature, do answers to problems come to you?
9. Do you have dreams that give you information or solve problems?
10. Have you ever had a dream or premonition of a future event that later occurred?
11. Have you ever "heard" the answer to a problem?
12. Do you prefer to skip the directions when putting something together and it always turns out fine?
13. Are you aware of a buzzing, tingling, or itchy feeling on your forehead or top of your head?
14. Are you constantly generating ideas for projects and creative pursuits?
15. Do you prefer to take the path less traveled and do things your way rather than the conventional way?
16. Have you ever seen something in your mind's eye, like a vision of an event, before it happened?
17. Do you get vibes about people that turn out to be true?
18. Do you have an uncanny knack for finding your way without maps or a GPS?
19. Are you aware of a certain faith and trust that you will always be okay no matter what?
20. Do you pick up on the emotions of the people around you?

Give yourself five points for each affirmative answer.

If you scored:

0–25: you may be living in your head too much. Do all the exercises in this book. Time to start paying attention to the intuitive signals you receive.

26–50: Your intuition is active, but a bit of practice with the exercises in the book could kick you into the next level.

51–70: You are probably aware that you are quite intuitive and have already been working on developing your abilities.

71 and above: You are very sensitive and could become quite psychic with a little practice.

So how did you do? Do you need some improvement or are you "there" already? Regardless, reading and doing the exercises in this book will open you up much further to receive intuitive guidance.

<u>Chapter One</u>

Meet Your Intuition

"Follow your instincts. That is where true wisdom manifests itself."
—Oprah Winfrey

What is intuition?

Your intuition is the key to finding your purpose, living with passion and joy, and increasing your success in life. It is that inner voice that directs you in times of need and reveals the unexpected solution to a problem that appears just when you need it. It's also that synchronistic phone call from a friend who says they have a connection to hook you up with the perfect job you have been dreaming of getting. It's all of that and more.

Following your intuition is that "knowing" inside that you are on the right path. It's that knowing that says, "It's time to leave this place" or thing. It says, "Go here and do this." It's that little voice that nags at you over and over until you listen. The one you hear for years and then, one day, you say, "Enough already!" When you decide to listen and follow this directive, the whole world opens up to you.

Your intuition is also your connection to Greater Intelligence. Some call it God, the creator, the "collective unconscious," the Universal Mind,

1

or the Divine Mind. What you call it doesn't change the fact that it exits and is so much smarter than we humans are. After all, this intelligence keeps the planets in orbit, the Earth turning, and the seasons changing. Could we ever do anything like that? Never. Not even in a million years could our technology create solar systems and galaxies and the intricate and miraculous life forms we have here on Earth.

To have this available to you at all times is to have a genius advising you. Who wouldn't want that? Can you imagine having a friend or advisor with you at all times who knows the answers to everything? A friend who can advise you of what you need to do in each and every situation? What a fabulous friend to have!

I'm here to tell you that you *really* do have this friend who is with you at all times. This trusted friend will gladly impart any information that you ask for, as long as you are willing to listen. And, when you learn to listen to your intuition, there will be nothing you cannot do. You can do more than you have ever dreamed of and be all you ever dreamed of. You can live the most fantastic, fulfilling life you could ever imagine. In fact, your life will exceed your wildest expectations when you learn to listen to your intuition.

Your intuition will lead you to do things you never did before, go places you never had any inclination to go before, and you will meet people you never thought you could have had access to before. Your intuition will open doors that before were closed to you.

Why? Because connecting to your intuition puts you on the path you were meant to take in this life.

Intuition unlocks your destiny and is your guide

Learning to use your intuition is like receiving a map to get to where your heart's desire wants to go. The only difference is that this map is blank when you first get it. You need to fill it in step by step. When you connect to your intuition, each and every step is revealed to you. Then, as if by magic, the map begins to emerge before you. It's no longer blank. It's right there in front of you.

The only way to get back on the path of what your mission is in this life is to listen to your intuition.

Surely you have met people who clearly knew from an early age what they were supposed to do in life? They have a very strong connection to their inner guidance. For the rest of us to "know," we must learn to listen to our intuition to get back on the road that is meant for us.

Taking assessment tests are fine for identifying your strengths, but knowing your strengths will not help you find your most auspicious road in life. When I was younger I took a test that suggested I'd be a really great naval officer. I can tell you that I was not cut out for the military. I'm not good at taking orders, and I'm no good with living a regimented life. I'm happiest when I can live life as free as a bird. I like to make my own hours and do what I want, when I want. Does that sound like the mindset of a naval officer?

Today you have at your disposal a plethora of books and courses to help you discover your passion in life. Years ago people never talked about their passion. It was an assumption that you would get out of school, get a job, and support your family. There was no passion involved. However, our society has evolved since then.

We now believe, as a society, that work is supposed to be something we enjoy. We also believe it should be fulfilling and that we should feel good about the service we are offering to others. While not every single working person may agree, this way of thinking is considered mainstream.

Many people in midlife who have been working their whole lives have come to realize that working just for the sake of making money is not enough. They burn out in droves and, as a consequence, many have made midlife career changes. They are also telling their children that, in order to be happy and live fulfilling lives, they must focus on doing something that really interests them rather than doing something just for a pay check. This new mindset is now trickling down through society and changing the way we think about careers.

Just fifty years ago we would have laughed at the idea that work was supposed to be fulfilling, but no more. We are evolving. As we evolve, we change others around us. The ideas that were being laughed at then have become mainstream ideas accepted by the masses. That is what is meant by evolving; it is making progress.

I was meditating and doing yoga years before it became popular. My friends thought I was weird. Now, many of my friends meditate and practice yoga. What Western society thought was so "far out" back then is now in the mainstream. It has moved from the fringes inward.

Intuition is knowledge from within

Merriam-Webster defines intuition as "attaining direct knowledge or cognition without evident rational thought and inference."[1] The word comes from the Latin word *intueri*, which is often roughly translated as meaning to "look at from inside" or "contemplate." That is why it's called In-tuition.

Intuition is "knowing" something without any logical way of knowing, or getting a flash while in the middle of doing something that is the answer you have been looking for to solve a problem. It can also be that sense of foreboding you might have in your stomach or the feeling of butterflies you have just prior to learning about something disastrous happening to a member of your family. Right before 9/11 many people experienced uneasiness but, until this tragic event occurred, they had nothing to ascribe it to. Your intuition is another way of getting information from your environment aside from the five senses. It is your very own inner guidance system.

We live in an ocean of consciousness

We are all part of what Jung referred to as the "collective unconscious," what theologians and mystics call God, and what modern scientists call a "field consciousness"[2] or "global mind" This field holds the potential for everything that is expressed in the Universe. It is within and around everything that exists, both seen and unseen. This "field" can be compared to what it might be like for a fish living in the sea. We live in this field of consciousness and, just like the fish, we are entirely unaware of it. We don't see or feel it, but it encompasses the world we perceive.

We are neither separated from this source of creation and knowledge nor are we separate from all its creations. It might appear that we are separate from one another and that we are separate from this vast source, but that is an illusion. Each of us is a part of this field being expressed as an energy pattern within a physical body for our brief existence on this planet. We cannot separate ourselves from it anymore than a wave can separate itself from the ocean.

---

1   Merriam-Webster Online, s.v. "intuition," accessed July 23, 2011, http://www.merriam-webster.com/dictionary/intuition.

2   Radin Ph.D., Dean I., *The Conscious Universe: The Scientific Truth of Psychic Phenomena* (New York, Harper Collins Publishers, 1997) p. 173.

When you tap into your intuition, what you have really accessed is this field. Think of it as if it were the World Wide Web for conscious.

Psychic ability is an extension of intuition

When we receive psychic impressions, we are getting them through this field of conscious intelligence. We are connected to every living thing through this field. Even though we cannot see it, all life forms are actually part of this great tapestry. If we pull one thread (or living thing/species) out, we change the entire tapestry and energy pattern of the field.

Do you ever find yourself feeling down when you are around a person who is sad? That is because your energy field mingles with their field and you are picking up on their mood. That is how extrasensory perception works. You can intuit other peoples' energies. You don't need to be near them to pick up on it. All you need to do is think of the other person and your energy field can make contact with them through the field.

One common example of this is when you have a thought about another person come to you out of the blue and then you either see them or hear from them not long afterward. One day I was taking a walk and a friend of mine, with whom I hadn't spoken in a while, came to mind. I vowed to call her as soon as I got home, but something else came up and I forgot. The following day this friend called and said she'd been thinking of me. We had been on the same wavelength.

Time and space are illusions

Because we live on the Earth plane and are having a physical experience, we relate to everything from a physical perspective. This includes the dimensions of time and space, but that is a very a limited perspective. We are unlimited. We can get information about another person at a distance anytime—remember it's all contained on the "World Wide Web of consciousness." All we have to do is desire the information. No computers or other technology is necessary.

As you begin to work with your intuition, you will also find your psychic abilities increase. They overlap in many areas. For now, know that intuition is your own guiding connection to Greater Intelligence. Psychic ability is connecting to another person, place, or thing through the field of consciousness.

he source of intuition?

rce of our intuition is the field of consciousness, or what I re-
ater Intelligence. This is the field of intelligence that spans the
Earth and the entire Universe of which we are all a part. When we open
ourselves up to intuitive guidance, this is where answers come from.

The field or global mind is what connects us to intuitive guidance
and to one another psychically. It is how we can receive divine guidance
and information about another person, place, or thing that is not within
our sight or otherwise unknowable to us. When we request information
about things that we cannot see with our eyes, our consciousness is pro-
jected through the field to the subject of our inquiry, and we obtain the
information directly from their own energy field or aura. We are not limited to knowledge contained in our brains or by the confines of our bodies. Our consciousness is as expansive as the entire Universe and beyond.

All that it takes to reconnect to this vast storehouse of knowledge is
our intention and desire. It's always there just waiting for us to invite it to
work with us. This knowledge will never force itself on you. It will only
flow where there is an open door and an invitation. That is why your
intention is so important. Your intention to allow your intuitive guidance
to work for you is the invitation needed. It is the open door and invitation
that Greater Intelligence seeks.

So, the next time you need guidance in your life, speak to Greater
Intelligence and say that you are open and ready to receiving help and
guidance. Know that this field of intelligence is loving and nurturing and
will respond immediately to your invitation.

Why are we intuitive?

We were initially given this ability to help keep us safe in order for
our species to survive. When we were first walking upon the Earth, our
needs were much less complex. We needed shelter and food. We procre-
ated, and then we needed shelter and to be able to feed our newborns.
In order to survive in the harsh conditions in which early humans first
found themselves living, they had be aware of all kinds of danger. There
were dinosaurs and woolly mammoths to avoid. The world was a dangerous place. If a hunter didn't come home at night with his catch and
instead became the catch, his family might starve. Intuition in the form of

gut instincts were there to make sure our species survived and thrived.

Even today, these gut instincts come in handy. Can you imagine not being aware when someone walks up behind you? Or, imagine not sensing the presence of danger when walking to your car in a dark and empty parking lot? The information about the impending danger is sent to you via your body, which picks up subtle cues in your environment that your conscious mind is not aware of. You were too preoccupied looking for your car keys to have seen that person approaching you from behind. Suddenly, the hairs on the back of your neck stand up, your back arches, and you feel the presence of someone behind you. You quickly unlock the door, jump in your car, drive away to safety, and stop to call the police on your cell phone. Without your intuition alerting you to danger, you could have been mugged, or worse.

Your intuition has evolved just as our species has evolved. We evolved and became much deeper thinkers with more complex needs. As we evolved, so did our intuition. Our intuition can now be used to answer questions we have in our lives. It can solve problems and give us information in order to make better decisions.

When you use your intuition today, you are able to gain the wisdom you need to navigate today's complex world much more than was needed by early man.

Why develop your intuition?

Intuition is the only way to connect to your authentic self and your true calling, your reason for being here at this time. While taking apititude tests might identify your strengths and what jobs you could do well at, nothing else will inspire you like getting in touch with your intuition. Simply choosing a profession because you are good at it is simply not enough. When you connect to your calling intuitively, you will feel alive and excited about what you are doing.

The beauty of intuition is in its simplicity. You don't need a lot of electronic gadgets, training, or money to start accessing the wisdom of your intuition. It's always been there waiting for you to open the door to it and invite it in. It flows from Greater Intelligence, to which we are all connected, right through you. It is the power animating your physical body, the power that inspires you with genius, enlivening you with enthusiasm for life and joy. It is also the power to steer you in the direction of your dreams.

If you feel stuck or suffer from lack enthusiasm for life, this book will help you reconnect to the source of your inspiration. You will learn to feel alive again. You will become authentically *you* again. You will learn to find joy and meaning and to be of service to others when you reconnect to your intuition. You will finally know your true purpose and begin to live with passion!

How would you feel if you were in the last days of your life and looked back and realized that you hadn't completed this mission? What if you knew you had wasted your life on the wrong pursuits? What could you possibly do about it at this point? Not much. But you have a choice to start now to reconnect to your intuition and turn your life around — before all the sand has poured from the hourglass. You don't want to waste another day, do you? Time is the only thing we can never get back. Once it's gone it's history. Why waste another precious moment on an unfulfilling life doing something you really dislike?

What if you could wake up every day with a spring in your step and energy that carries you easily and joyfully through your day? And what if you loved your life? Wouldn't that be the greatest feeling ever? To live a sensational and meaningful life you have got to find that one "thing" that you were meant to do in order to connect to that boundless source of energy and joy. You have got to do it now — not tomorrow or next week. Now is the time, before it's too late.

Think of the leaders and role models you admire. Don't you want to have the enthusiasm and zest for life that they have? What would it feel like to know your true purpose and to work with passion each and every day? To know your purpose and do what you love is the greatest gift you can give yourself. Aren't you tired of waiting?

I'm here to tell that you can have a brilliant and fulfilling life. All it takes is allowing your intuition to take the wheel. Stop trying to plan everything and every little detail. Stop fooling yourself into thinking you are in control of your life in its present mode, because you are not. Right now you are being batted around like a rowboat in a stormy sea by all the dilemmas and dramas in your life. Can you see that you are not in control? You are just reacting to everything that comes along in your life; that is not really living.

When you partner with your intuition you will have more control and better tools at your disposal. The guidance you will receive from your intuition will lead you to places you never dreamed of and you will discover abilities you never knew you had. You will meet people with whom you never would have expected to associate—those who will help and assist you. You will venture down roads you never knew even existed. Intuition is *that* miraculous. It is the light in the sky leading you when you weren't sure what to do next and illuminating the next door through which you were meant to walk.

The benefit of becoming your authentic self

Your authentic self is the universal you—the person you always thought you could be. It is your full and unbridled potential and who you really are at your core before your fears and beliefs about what is really possible reined in this brilliant reality. It's the pearl of your own private universe hiding within you. And it's been waiting there for you to discover it all this time. This is the gift of tapping into your intuition. Your intuition will guide you to where you are supposed to go next. Let yourself be in touch with it. Let it tell you what the next steps are.

Your authentic self is the source of your brilliance. When you know who you really are and stay true to what supports your authenticity, your life will flow with ease. We have all had moments of brilliance. But getting in touch with the source of your brilliance and staying connected will make you shine every day. Intuition allows everything to flow smoothly for the completion of your goals. Without it, you are on your own, out there in the dark without a beacon of light to guide you.

To develop your intuition is the best thing you can ever do for you and for your family. Developing your intuition can take you to that next big thing where you discover a new product or service that will be of great service to people. It will give you the brilliance to create the new business you have been dreaming of and affirm your life purpose. It will supply the ideas and people to support you in any endeavor you choose to undertake.

Why I wrote this book

The reason I'm so intent on teaching how you to follow your intuition is because I learned through experience: ignoring mine led to many poor decisions. I was pretty unhappy until I started listening to my intuition. I was an intuitive advising others, but I was not taking my own intuition seriously. I had a strong urge to leave corporate America and create my own business based around my writing and readings, but I resisted, choosing instead to hang onto to the safety of a secure job. When I had the opportunity to leave that job and change my life I did. But, when things got rough, instead of remaining calm and trusting that my intuition was leading me in the right direction, I ran back to the safety of my former career.

It's taken me twelve years to get back on track again. Had I only listened to my intuition, I would not have had to start over to build the life I had been dreaming of. Safety and financial security are important parts of our lives. But having money should never be the dream to which you aspire—only the by-product of following your heart and intuition.

When you base your life solely on gaining financial security, you end up doing everything for the wrong reasons. You are not connected to the joy that inspires you; instead, you are only connected to the outcome (making or having money) of what you are doing. That makes everything you do feel like a chore. There is no passion for your job, service, or business; it's just a grind. And when problems arise you're likely to give up; whereas, if you have a passion for what you're doing, you have the drive to see it through despite the challenges. You have got to be about loving your work first; the money will come later.

The work you do has to invigorate you, excite you. It has to be your "great obsession." You won't find your great obsession until you first let go of thinking about money. Money is just the visible sign that your work is needed, valued, and of service to the world. To listen to your intuition is to be inspired and to find your purpose. Your true purpose is the thing that you can't wait to get up in the morning and start doing.

What is the Intuition Principle?

The Intuition Principle is the concept that within you exists an innate technology, your intuition, capable of both guiding you to and attracting to you the life and happiness you've always dreamed of. By training your mind to go within to access your intuition you broaden your connection to all life, expanding your capacity for empathy and compassion that activates its full power as both a navigational device and homing beacon for your desires. Your intuition is the me-

dium through which Greater Intelligence communicates and orchestrates events in order to assist you in acquiring solutions to your every problem, achieving your highest potential, discovering your life purpose, and sharing these gifts and talents in loving service to help mankind—in effect, bringing the entire world to you.

You are here for a purpose. Each of us is here to use our special talents in our own unique way to help ourselves and the world.

The Intuition Principle is the backbone of our success in life. Without this fundamental connection to our intuition, we will miss the directions for the twists and turns we need to take to get to our destination. The intuitive guidance we receive is the key to getting the instructions, directions, and solutions we need in order to fill in the map we need to follow.

Without this map we are lost. We are afraid of taking the next steps, since we are unsure of which way to go; the atmosphere appears dark and stormy to us. When we learn to tune into our intuition the path will become clear. The Intuition Principle will lead us easily and effortlessly toward our destination.

This purpose allows us to express all the talents and gifts we were blessed with in this life. When we don't use these talents and gifts we find ourselves frustrated in life. We are not allowing these wonderful abilities to stream out of us and to be shared by the world. This creates a lot of pent-up frustration. We may not even realize why we are so frustrated. We might even feel anger or envy toward those individuals who are expressing the very gifts we have within ourselves—those we have yet to fully realize within ourselves.

We might even question why we are stuck in jobs we hate and work with people with whom we can't relate, when some people seem to find something they love to do and appear to love their lives. The answer is that we are either afraid to listen to our intuition and take that leap of faith, or we truly have not heard our intuition our whole lives. Learning to hear our intuition is easy to remedy with training, but overcoming the fear of listening to it when we have heard it and ignored it our whole lives is harder.

When we ignore our intuition, we would rather play it safe. Ignoring the call of our intuition will cause it to fester inside until we deal with it. Just because we choose not to act on our intuition doesn't mean it isn't there. Not acting on intuitive guidance and living our true purpose is the reason for much of our anger and frustration. Our fear of acting limits our lives and our growth. But jumping off the cliff in an act of faith and fearlessness actually opens the door to many rewarding experiences.

The Universe rewards us for following our intuition; we discover more opportunities for success, and with more ease and effortlessness in finding our way.

When we are scared, we are actually hiding from our fate. When we hide, we miss out on a sensational and successful life because we are too scared to take control. We have to step up and out in order to get the prize. That is why you see leaders and entrepreneurs getting so much attention. They stand out because they have succeeded in doing what 99 percent of the population is afraid to do. If you want to be a leader or an inspiration to others, you have to be able to take this leap of faith.

By having the courage and fearlessness to jump off this cliff, you allow the wind currents to pick you up and carry you to new places. When you go off-road you never know what adventures you will encounter; that excites the entrepreneur and scares the common person. The same events are seen differently by different individuals. That is the secret. If you see this as an opportunity, it becomes one. If you see it as a scary thing that you should avoid, you will avoid it and stay in your safe little rut all your life. You have to leap! It's the only way to freedom in this life.

By taking this leap of faith to rely on your intuition, you free yourself to go beyond the limits of your own personal knowledge. The truth is we are spiritual beings within human bodies. Our consciousness is not limited to this dimension simply because our spirit has donned a suit of flesh. We can reach out to other dimensions whenever we choose and get help and guidance. Through the power of intuition we are given a lifeline and direct connection to dial out of this dimension when we need help. The line may not seem as clear as it could be in the beginning, but that is only from lack of use. We have to practice and keep the line open by dialoguing with our intuition if we expect to hear anything clearly. Once we begin to tap into our intuition, we will establish a good connection.

The point is to place those calls early, listen to the answers we receive, and act on them. That is how we will see the map of our next steps materialize, and that is how we will rise above the limitations of the dimension we live in. We are not limited by time or space as we have all been conditioned to believe in our three-dimensional world. These conclusions are only illusions. We are pure spirit and cannot be held back by this dimension, but we have to discover this to know it's true. The way to discover this is to tap into intuition. When intuition guides you, you will rise above the conditions of this world. You will not be affected by the limitations that constrain others. You will become the multi-dimensional being you really are. And you will stand out and apart from others because of your guts and vision. Your vision will be limitless. Where others see obstacles you will see only exciting challenges.

We are here to learn these lessons, but very few of us do. We are here to learn that we are unlimited, multi-dimensional beings. We are here to learn that we can solve any problem and face any challenge so long as we have faith and the guidance of our intuition behind us to navigate this material world. We are here to learn that all of us are in the same boat when we come here and that we should love and help one another. One of the reasons people turn to crime and to hurting others is because, deep down, they are scared. They don't know that they are supported and loved by the Universe. They think they are alone and have to "fight and claw" their way out of everything when, actually, it's very much the opposite.

The more you are of service to others, the more you will also benefit. Those who do help others have overcome the basic fears that set in from believing that we are separate from one another. Seeing each other as we do in different bodies reinforces the illusion that we are separate. In actuality, each of us is very much a part of the energy and intelligence that makes up the ocean of consciousness pervading our Universe. We are here to reawaken those memories of our oneness and constant connection to our source. The way to do that is by using our intuition.

With the help of our intuition we will once again hear the truth about where we came from and why we are here. Our intuition keeps us connected to the other dimensions to which we will eventually return. If we don't "call and say hello" on a regular basis, we run the risk of losing touch with it. Our relationship will grow distant and we will begin to feel alone and unsupported. When we have a strong connection, we will always have support and a source of strength and comfort upon which to draw. When we face challenging circumstances in our lives, we will be able to turn to intuition for help, comfort, and guidance. That is why we have our intuition in the first place! If we didn't need it, we would not have been designed with this faculty.

The Intuition Principle reawakens your connection to your true spiritual nature

Your intuition is your lifeline to wisdom and guidance. It is a source of comfort and assistance in troubling times. It is there to remind you that your human life is only temporary and that you will return to the ocean of consciousness someday. It is there to make you aware that you need to remain lighthearted and not take this all so seriously—to play and have fun with the experience of being human. Enjoy the fruit that this life has to offer. Taste life and really live.

Don't cower in the corner, afraid of your own shadow and of all the things that can go wrong. If you do, you will have wasted this exquisite experience. Get out there and live fully. Enjoy every moment of your life. Don't waste it doing things you hate for a living. Do what you love and, if you don't know what that is, tap into your intuition: the answers will come.

Don't live your life in fear. When you live your life in fear, you have failed this mission. You will never achieve liftoff in the ride of your life if you are scared of life. When you left the safe, warm womb of spirit and entered the Earth's atmosphere, you were excited about the opportunity to experience life as a human being. Something happened when you were fully clothed in your suit of flesh: you lost that sense of excitement and fearlessness. Now you are just playing it as safe as possible until your time runs out. That is not really living. You have to take advantage of this wonderful life that you have been given. You have to take in as much life as you can while you are here; otherwise, you have wasted the opportunity.

People who listen to their intuition are living fully. People who are living their mission find great success and enjoyment of all the great gifts and abundance this three-dimensional world has to offer. They will leave here richer for their experiences.

Enrichment through experiences, not riches, is the goal

We are immensely enriched by our earthly experiences; this is how we gain wisdom. For some people, though, enrichment has become the pure pursuit of "riches." When we are connected to our intuition, we no longer feel driven to spend our lives amassing huge stockpiles or sessions in order to feel secure. We feel secure and supported, rather, by knowing we have the guidance we need to surmount any obstacle.

Our security comes from within through our intuition, not from things outside of us. Developing your intuition liberates you from the viscous cycle of needing to acquire more and more possessions. It is also the secret of how your intuition attracts all that you desire to your life. When you know that you will always have everything you need and that it will appear just when you need it, you no longer have to create a life that revolves around acquiring more and more. You are free from the cycle that enslaves you to working for the sake of maintaining your possessions. Once you no longer "need" so much to feel secure, you will find abundance continually streaming into your life easily and effortlessly anyway.

Finding life's instruction manual

The Intuition Principle reinforces that we were not sent here without any instructions. The instructions came with us. They are encoded within us; all we have to do to access them is to listen. When we live in fear of "making mistakes" and play small we actually turn down the volume on this guidance. Our fears begin to cut the connection to this source energy and, as a result, our inner light begins to dim. When our inner light fades we lose enthusiasm for life and can no longer make a productive contribution to the world. Our fear actually denies the world of our greatness and the potential solutions we might have contributed to making the world a better place. We actually owe it to our human family to allow our light to shine as brightly as possible. We owe it to them to live as big as our dreams allow us to live in order that we might make the valuable contribution that we came here to make.

Learning from our mistakes

I always had the feeling that something was wrong with the way I was living. The belief system I grew up around was based in fear. I was taught to "be careful" not take too many risks and to play it safe. While the message I was received was that you couldn't trust the big bad world out there, I felt instinctively that this was wrong. I didn't want to believe it was a big bad world out there.

I had this desire inside me to jump up on a table and dance with abandon and really enjoy my life, but on the outside I felt shackled by the fear that had been instilled in me. I lived my life playing by all the rules. I got a good job, grew into my career, and was able to support myself. I lived well, but I was so unhappy. Why? I started to realize that it had to do with not fulfilling my true calling. Making money was great, but where was the joy in my life? I started to pursue what I loved and my life got better, but I was still too afraid to let go of my security blanket, which I thought was having money. I hadn't yet figured out that it was the need for security that was holding me back.

I thought if I had money and possessions first, I could then go for what I wanted and be safe and happy. But I learned it doesn't work like that. You have to go for what you want first and then the money and possessions will come. You have to have the security *within* yourself first or no amount of money will ever be able to make you feel safe.

What I realized is that we are all living our lives in a backward motion. We are approaching our earthly experience all wrong. We aren't teaching our kids the right things. We are teaching them to go after possessions as a way to make them feel happy, fulfilled, and secure, when really all we are doing is setting them up for misery. They will never achieve happiness this way. All they will be doing is getting addicted to a cycle of chasing after material possessions to fill a need that those possessions can never fill. As soon as they get the newest possession they will tire of it and need to go out and get another thing to feel good again. And, the vicious cycle will continue.

As within, so without

In order to unearth the directions and map that are buried deep within you have to be willing to go out on a limb and take a chance. You have to be willing to risk all that security you think is so important in order to find out that the security is within you. In fact, the entire Universe is within you. Everything that you are looking for outside of yourself is already within you.

Learning this has freed me to be able to go achieve my dreams and to listen to my intuition. I am limitless and so are you. The fulfillment we seek in our lives is readily available when we leap headlong into the current in the river of life and allow ourselves to experience this journey fully. When we hold back out of fear and believe that we must control everything and play it safe, we will never fully experience the exquisite joy of living in this dimension. We will remain tethered to the shore and see only that which washes up, instead of reaching distant shores and immersing ourselves fully in new cultures and tasting all there is to taste on our journey.

Are you ready to jump in and begin the most exciting journey of your life?

<u>Chapter Two</u>

Live an Intuitively Inspired Life

"The only important thing is intuition.

– Albert Einstein

When you follow your intuition you will live an inspired life

This is the foundation of my philosophy and my advice for anyone who is looking to live a significant and successful life.

What does living a "significant and successful life" look like?

A significant life means that your work is centered on service to others; to be successful means that your life works and is balanced in all facets.

Successful doesn't necessarily mean great wealth, although it can. Balance is the key here. However, it does mean that:

- You are happy and enjoy your life

- You have healthy relationships and relate to others with empathy and compassion

- You are able to give as well as receive

- You take care of your body and eat sensibly and exercise

- You are devoted to your spiritual growth and have a daily spiritual practice that helps keep stress in check

- You are open to new ideas and constantly learning

- You live comfortably and have what you need to feed your family, pay your bills, and to save some money.

This is not to say that you will live a problem-free life—that is highly unlikely. You will, however, be better equipped to deal with challenges than the next person due to the substantial advantages that developing your intuition brings you.

The truth is that developing your intuition has many benefits to help you succeed in all areas of your life, such as:

- Stress Reduction
- Peace of mind
- Better focus
- Improved memory
- Decision-making
- Improved relationships
- Increased capacity for empathy and compassion
- Better health
- Increased luck
- Increased abundance
- More joy
- Body awareness
- Empowerment
- Ability to say "no" more easily
- Heightened creativity
- Problem solving skills
- Teaches you to think like a genius
- Discovery of your true purpose

This is why I recommend developing intuition and why I have made it the foundation of my own self-development.

How does developing intuition create so many benefits?

Stress reduction

Learning to listen to your intuition is learning to "go within." You must not only become more selective about the thoughts you "hear," but also learn how to slow down your thoughts so you really do "hear" them. This in and of itself reduces stress. The process of "listening" for your intuition reduces the "mind chatter" that contributes significantly to daily stress. You become relaxed as your mind calms down; this affects your body's physiological stress responses.

When you hear your thoughts—that is to say the *right* thoughts—and selectively filter out the self-defeating ones, you are also better able to reduce the inner conflict and stress. Most inner conflict results from negative or self-limiting beliefs that directly undermine the goals you are trying to achieve. Not listening to these negative thoughts, which reduces stressful inner conflicts, makes you more effective.

Recent scientific findings have shown that the brain has great plasticity[1] and can be retrained. This means that you can eliminate habitual negative or self-defeating thoughts. With practice and discipline you can carve out new neural pathways[2] in the brain, the path through which information travels from one region of the brain to another, based on positive and affirming beliefs that replace the old negative ones. By instilling a practice of listening for your intuition, you are retraining your brain to screen out the negative thoughts that repeat in a loop and to search instead for the life-affirming messages of your intuition.

---

1   Theresa Boyle, "The brain: changing the adult mind through the power of plasticity," Healthzone, July 30, 2010. http://www.healthzone.ca/health/mindmood/article/842511--the-brain-changing-the-adult-mind-through-the-power-of-plasticity?bn=1
2   Medical Glossary Online, s.v. "neural pathway," accessed July 24, 2011, http://www.medicalglossary.org/nervous_system_neural_pathways_definitions.html

Improves focus

This is the by-product of becoming selective and slowing down the internal thought process. As you become calmer—due to slowing the pace of thoughts—you are better able to focus on the task at hand.

You are no longer easily distracted from your focus by frantic thoughts about another matter. You are able to remain in the present moment, clear and attentive.

Improves your memory

As you learn to banish random thoughts, making less cluttered thinking a part of your daily life, you will find that you are better able to concentrate upon only one thing at a time; you remember things more easily and clearly. With discipline, the many hundreds of other thoughts you have swirling around in your mind recede to the background, allowing you to absorb and record the information upon which you are concentrating. With this type of focus memory is no longer a problem.

Improves decision-making

Regular practice of reducing mind-chatter improves the quality of your thinking. Without the interruption of non-essential thoughts you can take different scenarios related to your decision and focus upon them more intently from many angles to be sure you are making the right decision.

You are also more aware of subtle senses and feelings that arise during this process. These subtle senses and feelings are how your intuition guides you. When the mind is racing you miss these very subtle clues that are often just below the level of awareness. You can deliberately ask yourself a question pertaining to the decision at hand. Then, with your mind cleared of extraneous thoughts, you become aware of impressions, images, symbols, fleeting thoughts, and feelings that arise as a result. An out-of-control and stressed-out mind will not be fertile soil for an exercise such as this.

When you become more aware of the subtle feelings operating below your radar you will "know" whether or not you should get involved with a certain person. You will "know" if someone is not being truthful. You will be acutely aware that there is more to the story than someone is telling you. These senses are worth their weight in gold. How many times in your life have you said, "Why didn't someone warn me not to do that?" or "Why didn't someone warn me about going with this person?"

Improves relationships

When you learn to slow down your thinking, you also become slower at "reacting." Many problems in relationships arise due to "reacting." If you react on autopilot all the time, you won't think before you speak; that can hurt relationships. The quality of your thinking improves when you gain control over your mind. You will be more compassionate, kind, and sensitive in your responses if you are able to pause for a moment and think, instead of using your words as weapons.

In developing your intuition you become more tuned in to another person's emotions. This allows you to become aware of and deal with problems before they have gone too far. You become more open to registering the subtle feelings that usually fall beneath your radar. Registering these fleeting thoughts and feeling will alert you to brewing problems—such as changes in the behavior of another person—which you might have otherwise overlooked. You will get a nagging feeling that won't go away, or a sudden hunch that you ought to check in with friends close to someone you may be worried about. Used this way, intuition can prevent a small problem from becoming a major crisis, such as a spouse looking for emotional comfort elsewhere or children dabbling in drugs.

Increases the capacity for empathy and compassion

Developing your intuition expands your connection to all living creatures. By broadening this connection you begin to feel what others are feeling emotionally, whether they are happy or in pain. Thereby, you experience what it is like to walk in their "sandals." Once the channels of intuition are opened a heightened capacity for empathy, compassion, tolerance and understanding for others and all life automatically follows.

Improves health

When you learn to slow your thoughts by decreasing mind chatter you reduce stress levels. That ultimately improves your health. Your body's systems function in a more balanced manner. There are no huge spikes in harmful hormones that can exacerbate disease. You also become more in tune with your body. You are able to notice, perhaps for the first time, that when you eat certain foods your heart races, or you get a mild headache, which could indicate a possible food allergy. You might never have become aware of these subtle health cues if your thoughts were still jumbled and racing all the time. You will hear wisdom directly from the body's intelligence as to what it needs and craves for healthy living that otherwise would have been drowned out in the past. You listen when you hear the gentle promptings to call your physician over a stubborn ailment that won't go away, a small lump found in an abnormal place, or even when it's time to take a vacation and get away from unrelenting stress.

Heightens creativity

When you learn how to listen for your intuition, you will begin receiving "intuitive flashes" and "hunches" that contain unexpected gems you never would have thought of on your own. The process of slowing down thoughts creates a bigger space between them. This allows ideas and inspiration to get through. You are now registering thoughts and flashes of brilliance that before were operating beneath the level of your awareness. New ideas will materialize from out of nowhere, answers will come, and inspiration will manifest regularly when you are attuned to your intuition.

Boosts problem-solving

The ability to focus, take on a problem, and look at it with fresh eyes—from all angles and outcomes—allows the mind to take pieces from those different angles and put them together in a completely different way. The discipline of calming the mind allows you to be open to new solutions instead of replaying the same two or three options over and over again.

Increasing your reliance upon your intuition also gives you the confidence, after repeated successes, to know that if you instruct your mind to search for the solution it will find it. Beating your head against a wall with the same circuitous thoughts will never bring you innovative ideas. Intuition opens the well spring to a never-ending source of ideas.

We start thinking like geniuses

A genius is someone who is capable of accessing his or her mind more fully. Learning to use more of your intelligence is what developing intuition does for you. Increasing your ability to maintain a single-minded focus, a super-sharp memory, superior decision-making abilities, heightened creativity, a more open mind, and enhanced problem-solving skills gives geniuses their edge. When you use your intuition, you stretch the limits of your mind and create new neural pathways for thinking in this manner. That is what a genius does, and so can you.

Stop living in your head and get back in touch with your body

When you live in your head all the time you lose touch with your body. Your body is always speaking to you whether you know it or not. Your body is receiving thousands of sensory messages all day from your environment. If danger approaches, the hairs on the back of your neck stand up.

I will give you another example. Say you are rushing to meet a friend when just before you leave the house a strong feeling of nausea and anxiety comes over you. You get the sudden feeling that she is going to be late, but you brush it off. Eventually, the anxiety and nausea dissipate, but you wait and wait at the restaurant. Finally, your friend shows up and tells you she almost cancelled due to last-minute babysitter problems. You suddenly "remember" the brief discomfort you experienced in your gut. You wonder whether it was just your imagination. Or was it your intuition telling you not to rush?

In these examples your body is processing information for you outside of your conscious awareness. This is the reason you want to stop depending on your thinking mind all the time. You cannot hear or feel your intuition if you are always thinking. You have got to be in the moment. You have got to be fully present and aware of all the sensations that quickly flash through your body. Can you remember a time when you had a horrible sinking feeling in your gut, or butterflies in your stomach? You didn't know what to attribute it to until your niece called telling you that your sister had been in a car accident. As soon as you got the call the feeling subsided. That was your body registering the emotional impact of looming danger or a matter with which you should concern yourself; in this case, it was your sister's accident.

Once you begin to work with your intuition—if you desire it—the information will appear more frequently. Flashes of ideas or pictures will stream through your mind that will describe the event to go along with that feeling. The more you practice the less frequently you will have gut feelings arise for which you have no corresponding event—until you hear about what has taken place—to interpret them. That is how your body communicates with you.

In order to hear this wisdom you need to be squarely centered in your body. You need to stop living in your head and reconnect to the body. Start paying attention to the feelings you get and the sensations in your body. One good way to reconnect to your body is to place your hand on your abdomen whenever you are stressing out or need inner guidance. Purposely placing our hand on our body brings our awareness down from our heads back into the body.

In another example, say you call your father to tell him you are leaving in two weeks for a two-month sabbatical in another state and your father tells you that he isn't feeling well. You start to feel anxious. After the phone call you sit quietly. Putting your hands on your abdomen to get in touch with your "gut" you ask yourself, "Is my father seriously ill?" You get a sinking feeling: yes, he is. You call him the next day and ask him if he's made a doctor's appointment and you offer to go with him. This is where the wisdom of intuition comes into play. After a round of doctor's appointment and tests you discover you father has a terminal illness. You cancel all your plans and stick around for a few months to spend the most quality time with him you can. Thank goodness for your intuition.

Improves confidence

One thing I can say from experience is that learning to develop your intuition is the best way to develop more confidence. Can you imagine knowing that you have the ability to check whether a plan will work out before you spend the money on pursuing it? Or, can you think of a better way to know whether to allow your teen to go to that party where later police show up and all the kids are arrested? Having the ability to "know" builds confidence like nothing else. Don't get me wrong. There will be times when you are wrong—mostly when you are worried about something and your logical mind gets in the way by presenting your fears as an intuitive hunch—but, for the most part, you will be able to avoid disasters and wrong decisions by learning to rely on your intuition.

The confidence you gain will serve you well in so many areas of your life too. You will be able to speak your mind with conviction. You will be able to stand your ground with your kids, knowing that your decision is the best thing in this situation. You will never regret the time you put in to develop your intuition.

After having a few "hits," your confidence will begin to soar. It soars because you are now becoming "brilliant." Many people use that word, but what does being *brilliant* really mean? It means shining, standing out from the crowd, or having a light surrounding you that others can see. When you are brilliant it's because you are accessing Greater Intelligence. You are using every faculty available to you. You have a line right into an infinite intelligence feeding you the answers in life. These are the answers everyone else wishes they had. So, knowing you have this life line available to you all the time gives you tremendous confidence. You will find yourself doing things you had never dreamed you would have the moxie to do before.

Contributes to your prosperity

One of the other amazing benefits of developing your intuition is that it contributes to your overall prosperity and abundance. When you are tuned into your intuition you will know the right opportunity when it arises. There will be no hemming and hawing over it. You will know that this is the one to go for. You will be able to differentiate whether to take one job over another. You will know when a business opportunity is the one you have been waiting for. The moment it is presented to you there will be a "good" feeling about it. You will "see" in your mind's eye the opportunity playing itself out. You will see yourself being really successful at it. It will be because the Universe has sent you a direct message telling you that this is the chance you have been waiting for. All those months of false starts and investigating one opportunity after another will result in this one moment of truly knowing this is the right opportunity. It is really amazing how this works. You will be stunned at how you easily know that this particular opportunity is "it."

Once in this new profession, business, or job you will know immediately that you are on the right path because your success will flow almost effortlessly. That is what happens when you follow your intuition. Guidance from Greater Intelligence puts you in the right place, a place that you are supposed to be in for your continued growth and evolution.

In order to make sure you follow this path, the Universe line
that affirm you are on the right path, making it much easier
course. Don't you want things to come more easily? Wouldn'
to have the backing of the entire universe behind you? What n
you ask for? The intelligence that created you—that which can solve any
problem—is now working for you. Wow!

The thing about following your intuition and having the Universe
behind what you are doing is that everything flows beautifully. People
come out of nowhere to help you. Doors open that you could have sworn
would remain closed to you.

When you try to do it your way—without the benefit of your intuition
helping you—it's hard. You have to work twice as hard, sometimes even
three times as hard. You need to solve all the problems that arise yourself. There is no serendipity, or "fortunate coincidences or synchronicity, meaning meaningful coincidences," in your life. People don't appear
when you need them, answers don't come up just when you start looking, and doors don't magically open to you. This is because you don't
have the Universe behind you feeding you the answers you need at just
the right moment. You have to come up with all of it by yourself. If you
haven't forgotten, you are only human.

When you rely on the Universe to guide you through your intuition,
you possess the power of the mighty heavens and an infinite store of
wisdom your small human brain cannot even begin to comprehend. So,
again, why wouldn't you want to tap into your intuition? It's not that
hard—it just takes a bit of practice.

We become luckier

Using intuition allows us to become luckier. Richard Wiseman, Ph.D.,[3]
stated in his 2003 book, *The Luck Factor* (Hyperion), that people who rely
more on intuition create more fortunate circumstances in their lives. He
discovered that luckier people were open to new experiences, which re-
sulted in their benefitting from more opportunities.

When you put the benefit of intuition on your side you will know
what to do and when to do it. You will be able to take chances on things
more easily because you will have built up greater confidence than those

---

3   Richard Wiseman, Ph.D., *The Psychology of Luck*, Richard Wiseman dot
com, http://www.richardwiseman.com/Luck.shtml

who don't use intuition. Your experiences with intuition will bolster your confidence. Knowing that you have the Universe behind you, you will take a risk when someone else may not. When you take risks you increase the chances of being lucky. You put yourself out there. You don't sit idly by and wonder if you should do something; you go and meet people. When you put yourself out in the world your odds go up for running across that person you can partner with, or that idea or opportunity that surely wouldn't have come to you had you been home wondering, waiting, and wishing.

You become exponentially luckier than people who are not in touch with their intuition. You have such an attitude of confidence that people and lucky circumstances seem to be attracted to you as if you are a magnet. That is why intuition also increases your abundance and prosperity. It all works together to make you a mover and a shaker with whom people want to be involved; they want some of your brilliance to rub off on them. Believe me, you cannot begin to imagine the fortunate circumstances that will arise when you begin to tap into your intuition.

You learn to say no and develop better boundaries

Another thing you will find when you develop your intuition is that you will start being able to say no. You now know what your mission is—what activities serve that mission and which ones do not. You will find yourself saying no to things you used to be uncomfortable turning down. You will be able to say no to those extracurricular activities that served no purpose for you but just took up a lot of time. You will be able to say no to your family, husband, or child when you really want to say no, instead of feeling guilty all the time. Feeling guilty is just plain crazy. All that happens is that you start to build up resentments. When you say no when you truly want to, you feel stronger inside and you feel that you can more fully take charge of your own life. When you learn to say no you become aware that you can create the future you desire.

Become empowered

Learning when to say no and losing the guilt is empowering. You feel that you are in control of your life. You are no longer tossed about like a small boat on a rough sea. You can decide when and if you want to do something and if it is beneficial for you to do. If you keep doing things that are only good for others, you start to lose respect for yourself and feel like a doormat.

But, when you start to rely on intuition, you start to stand up straight and take charge of your life. You can do things for others, but it will be for the right reasons. You will help others because you really want to and because the person genuinely requires your help. When you give in because of guilt or feelings of obligation you are not helping them for the right reasons. When you offer to assist someone begrudgingly, you send out vibes that others pick up. Just like your own intuitive cues, they sense your reluctance and feel uncomfortable with your help. They pick up that you don't really want to be there, too. So, make sure when you agree to do something you do it for the right reasons.

One other thing about always being there to help others is that you can become a nursemaid, helping others do the things they need to learn to accomplish on their own. Your child might not need you to do his homework with him every night if what you are doing is solving the math problems for him, right? Your family member may not really need you to run his or her errands or finish the chores he or she promised to do but has come to rely on you to complete. You are really not doing them any favors by doing everything for them, now are you?

Reduces worry by increasing peace of mind

Another great benefit of intuition is that you stop worrying so much. You know that the solutions to your problems will appear. You have proof from your prior experience to know that it does happen like this when you let go and trust. You remain calmer than others even in a crisis. You have the confidence from your past experience to know that things will work out eventually.

You become the go-to person; you are the calm center in the storm. You have a peace of mind others envy. You have a sense about things. You have the answers. You are a calming force on others. You don't seem to worry like other people. You stand out as exceptional. You develop a sage-like presence; your wisdom is recognized by others because of your calmness and ability to know the answers and what to do when—all in a humble and selfless way.

Increases joy

You become joyful about everything. Your life flows so beautifully now. You have every reason to be joyful. You have reached a place where you remain centered, even under the direst of circumstances; remaining centered is the secret to being joyful. Being joyful is different from being "giddy" with happiness, or elated or on a high. Being joyful is deep and profound appreciation for everyone and everything in your life. You are no longer flustered by life's events. You remain in a very steady emotional state of mind where you are not swinging wildly from one extreme to the other. You don't have those manic highs and lows. You are just joyful and happy. This state of mind creates even more luck, abundance, happiness, and fortunate coincidences. In order to be joyful you have to live in the present moment. Your mind is not off on some tangent in the future or off reliving a past event. You are serene, calm, and accepting of what is, seeing the beauty of what is. That is one of the most extraordinary benefits of intuition. You get to "be here now."

If not now, when? When you really stop to think about it, reliving the past or endlessly fantasizing about the future isn't really living. You only have this moment. Time is the only thing you cannot get back, right? You can take a class over if you fail, but you won't ever get the time back that you put into the course. It's gone.

People who live in the past or the future all the time are disconnected from their environment. They are so immersed in what happened already, or what they fear may happen, that they miss everything that is going on around them. A racing mind that never stops can lead to being clumsy, always bumping into things, or falling down because they aren't "here." They aren't aware of their surroundings. So, take care not to shut out your intuition. Nurture it and treasure it. It's your golden ticket to a better life in every sense of the word.

Discover your true purpose

One of the awesome things about tapping into your intuition is also discovering your purpose. You cannot truly know who you are or what you were meant to do until you are connected to Greater Intelligence. You come into this life with a plan based on how to utilize your talents and abilities to learn to be the best you can be. But unearthing that plan can be difficult and can cause you to spend way too much time stumbling around in the dark trying to find your way back to the path you are supposed to be on.

By learning to develop your intuition early in life, you can save yourself years of agony and mistakes. One thing that happens when you are connected to your intuition is that you feel directed to undertake certain courses of action—unlike someone who flounders and tries many different things but never finds the one thing that "fits." You are aware of your interests and you allow them to pull you toward suitable activities.

I'll give you an example. Let's say you are connected to your inner wisdom at a young age and drawn to play the clarinet while in elementary school. You stick with it even through high school when kids might be making fun of you. If you don't have a strong sense of intuition, you could be swayed by peer pressure to give it up in high school. Then you may end up going to business school because your logical mind tells you this is "right thing to do." Nonetheless, you can't shake the feeling of being a round peg in a square hole.

In your late forties you start to learn about the importance of intuition and you pick up the clarinet again. You wonder why you ever stopped. You start to play with some jazz musicians on the weekend at a small club. Then you find that playing the clarinet is all you can think of doing. You have to find a way to do this, but now you are stuck. You have amassed a big house, a mortgage, and all the other expenses that come with having a business career. How can you give it all up? How can you just walk away?

You are frantic. You need to feel connected to your artistic side. You need to have that expression of creativity flowing through you on a daily basis. You decide to sell everything and quit your job to make music before it's too late. Everybody thinks you are crazy, that you are having a midlife crisis, but you do it anyway. You have reached a stage in your life where you don't care what people think anymore. (Besides, there is a little voice inside that keeps egging you on and reassuring you that all will be well.)

You spend the next five years playing with your jazz group, cut an album, and then end up the subjects of someone's documentary film about midlife career changes. The publicity causes your jazz career to skyrocket. Now, you are living your dream. You may not be making the huge bucks you were making before in business but the money that is coming in now that you have become known is pretty decent. You are in heaven every day. You get out of bed and know that you are living your dream, walking the path you were supposed to be on. You know that this is the way your life was supposed to turn out. Thank goodness you listened to your intuition and went for it.

Now when you speak to your old colleagues they are all so envious of you. The ones who thought you were crazy are now your biggest fans. Boy, what a turnaround, huh?

Developing your intuition has many practical applications and, while not all have fairy tale endings, it can lead you to places you have never dreamed of going if you listen. You won't get there by doing the same old thing over and over. And you won't get there by listening to the advice of others. You have to take your own road. Your intuition will help you to stand tall and take chances and be who you were meant to be in this life.

You will stand out from the crowd because you have the vision to follow your gut. You will become a leader and a role model for others as one who has the courage of conviction and foresight to do things your own way. Maybe that is just what we need in this world: more leaders who have the guts to follow their intuition and not the pack. That could be you? Who knows?

Your intuition is your connection to the natural world

You didn't always live in your head all the time. When the pace of life was slower and more connected to nature, humans were less distracted and relied on their intuition much more. Think of the way Native Americans hunted and tracked animals. That was not only an art—reading the clues that animals left behind—but it was also an intuitive exercise. Think about it. If you learned to read every broken twig and crushed blade of grass, do you think you would be lucky enough to catch your dinner every day if you didn't also rely on your intuition?

What has happened is that we have lost touch with our intuition due to all sorts of other activities that commandeer our minds unceasingly: smart phones, computers, and television programs. We are literally distracting ourselves to death! In the process of all this distraction we are plundering and exploiting our planet; no one has really stepped in to stop it. We are all so stuck in our heads that we haven't heard our innate intelligence crying out to us: "Do I really need a bigger house?" "Do I really need more stuff?" "Do I need such a big car?" In the meantime our environment is suffering because of our "need" to purchase more and more things.

Indigenous people all over the world, who are still living apart from the "civilized" world, condemn these practices. They are crying out to us to wake up and hear the messages that Mother Earth is sending us: "Stop it. You are killing me, and it's going to kill you in the long run as well!"

What you need is to reconnect to intuition in order to become conscious of your oneness again. When you are aware of the unity of all life, you cannot plunder and pollute the Earth and decimate the animal life living on the planet. Are you aware that there is a huge mass of plastic swirling around in the North Pacific Ocean? Sea animals die when they are entangled and mutilated in it. Reconnecting to our intuition would change the culture from greed and violence to love and tolerance.

How did we let this happen?

We became disconnected from our hearts and our intuition. We allowed our rational minds to "lie" to us. When we live in the mind we can rationalize anything and make it seem all right. But really we "know" on a deeper level that this is not all right. How can it be? How can it be okay to allow tons of plastic to go down the sewers and out into the oceans? Who can really say, without lying, that this is acceptable behavior? Only the ego or rational mind would say things like, "Well, in order for man to progress, we have to be willing to sacrifice a little of our planet here and there. It's okay because we'll figure out a way to fix it later."

Can you see how this kind of logic is a lie? Can you see how this has led each and every one of us to buy into this myth? We have been hypnotized, believing that we can all have big houses, tons of clothes, cars, and gadgets, and spend our lives shopping every Saturday. Then we can discard what we have lost interest in and put it in giant landfills where all kinds of toxic substances seep into the earth and groundwater. Is this not insanity?

When you do things that you know deep inside are wrong your ego mind will rationalize to make you feel okay with it. I'm just as guilty as the next person. That is what the ego does: it rationalizes. It can come up with great excuses and also great lies to keep us feeling okay with things. So, when I say we need to start connecting to the world and each other through our hearts again, I'm saying it for a reason and that reason is to save the planet and save our species.

Developing your intuition will benefit the world

The time is now to help heal our world and our planet. When you learn to tap into your intuition, you will know innately what is needed to keep you on the right path. You won't go off on tangents that aren't meant for you (like my example about the fellow who has a business career rather than a jazz musician's career). You will find that you are happy with what you already own, rather than having to continually acquire more. This will help save precious resources in the world.

Having what you need and enjoying what you have is a wonderful part of the human experience, but an insatiable desire for more will rob you of the joy of feeling "satisfied" with your life. Living in a constant state where "enough is never enough" is a source of unhappiness. When the ego drives us to seek more, more, more it is because we feel empty inside. And when we feel empty we are unhappy.

Acquiring lots of things is really a substitute for the excitement you feel when you live your purpose. But you don't know that until you start living your purpose. You fill yourself up with things because you still feel unfulfilled. When you are living with purpose you don't get hung up on having things, you would rather have experiences. You can't take material wealth with you, as everyone knows from hearing this over and over, yet so many people continue to amass huge stockpiles of physical wealth: cars, houses, and huge wardrobes. Getting in touch with your intuition doesn't mean you will suddenly have the urge to give up all your stuff and live in a tent, but you will become more aware of what drives you to acquire the stuff you *think* you need. Do you really need so much stuff? Probably not. This all comes from confusing your inner voice with your ego's voice.

The ego is always fearful that it doesn't have enough. It will prompt you to fear you don't have enough food, money, or possessions to survive. The ego's voice is always based in fear and is always behind an "us versus them," or "mine versus theirs" mentality. When you put a lid on the ego's voice and tap into your intuition, your confidence soars. You realize that you don't need so much. You realize you can exist and be perfectly happy with less. You start to wake up from the collective dream we have all been having that in order to be happy you have to constantly strive to have more and live bigger. You see yourself as complete and whole just as you are. You see the authentic you; that is the real you that you start living for.

When we all start doing that en masse, our planet will have a fighting chance of survival. Right now there are still too many people clamoring for the Western lifestyle. Western culture has been exported all over the world thanks to satellite television and the Internet; virtually everyone has been exposed to this lifestyle. It's an explosion this planet just cannot sustain. We must start returning to our natural state of using our innate intelligence once again or our planet doesn't have a fighting chance.

Intuition expands your consciousness

When you begin to use your intuition more and rely less on the rational mind, a huge shift in your consciousness occurs. Along with this huge shift is a reordering of your priorities. You see why you are here. You see how you have veered off course. You see that you have to change. You want to change and discover that the change is effortless.

You begin to see the folly of wars and aggression in our society. You see that the only reason you are here is to learn to love unconditionally. You want to be a beacon for others to get this message out and help wake others up to this great realization of our true purpose.

Once you have had a shift in consciousness you cannot go back. You begin to base your decisions on what is good for the planet at large and what is good for others, not just what is good you. This shift in consciousness is what will save the planet.

Developing our intuition is part of our evolution as a species

When you expand your consciousness, you are actively playing a role in your evolution. When you evolve, you begin to move away from the left-brain thinking of your past. With expanded conscious, we will become a more altruistic society. Violence will decline. People will be more willing to make decisions that are good for the whole of humanity rather than just for them. Humanity will return to its natural state of goodness and innocence.

When I say innocence I don't meet naiveté. I mean a state where you no longer are cynical about things. You have innocence when you don't laugh at other's misfortune and don't find it humorous to laugh at another's expense. A state of innocence is a good thing, trust me. It means you have evolved from being crude and rooted in your needy small self into being a big shining being of love. You are less egocentric and able to see the good in all people and all things.

Once the majority of society is made up of individuals inspired by intuition, a culture of creativity will be instilled. With this heightened creativity you can solve any problem that arises. You will be responsive rather than reactive to problems. You are also less likely to create problems due to your more creative nature. As you become more balanced and reliant upon your intuition, the life changes you go through will inspire someone else to follow in your footsteps. Then that person will inspire someone else.

Before we know it, intuitively inspired thinking will reach a critical mass. Society will reach the point where its collective consciousness will be at a tipping point. At this tipping point the intuitive thinkers will outnumber the non-intuitive thinkers. When this happens our society will take "one giant leap" in our evolution. The intuitive thinkers will be the ones in political positions changing laws and legislating for a better world. Corporations will be run differently. At this point there will be no going back. We will begin to see our world changing immeasurably for the better.

Developing your intuition is the most exciting thing you can do

Are you beginning to see that developing your intuition is the most exciting thing you can do and the most exciting way to live your life?

Inspiration will come through hearing the voice of your intuition; this inspiration will lead to miraculous coincidences and on toward your divine purpose. Signs will appear, synchronous events will arise, and coincidences will increase; you meet the persons you need to meet at the right time. You will learn to follow a hunch, read about just the very thing you need to do for your next step, or get a flash of intuition about the solution to a problem.

So don't wait. Learn to still your mind and allow the wisdom of your intuition to reveal your glorious path.

Get started now

To prepare for your exciting journey take out a sheet of paper and answer the following questions. The questions are designed to help you begin to get in touch with your intuition.

1. **Do you allow yourself to be influenced by what others say is right for you?** Take time to discover what your own values are. What is important to you? What principles do you choose to live your life by? What do you stand for? If you could be living your perfect life now, what would it look like? Gaining confidence and the courage of your convictions is vital to developing intuition. If you don't feel confident about your values you are going to second guess and discount your intuitive hunches all the time.

2. **Are you afraid to ask for help?** If you are facing problems in your life, talk about what you are going through with friends or family. Opening up is the first step in preparing your mind for receiving intuitive guidance. When you are closed off or defensive and not open to receiving help, it's a mindset that spills over to intuition. The closed mind will miss the subtle intuitive cues, too. What do you need help with now? Is all but one area of your life going well? Or, do you need help in several areas such as relationships, finances, career, spirituality, or health?

3. **Would you benefit from a few sessions of working with a coach or counselor?** Sometimes problems are just too big or overwhelming to you. You need an objective third party to help you sort things out, especially when the problem entangles your emotions. A coach or counselor can work with you until you have become more skilled at handling your problems. Working with someone can also help you to begin tuning into your intuitive wisdom as well.

4. **Do you take time to become quiet each day and go within?** Learn to still your mind with daily meditation and reflection. There is no way to hear the voice of your intuition if your mind chatter is con-

stant. Learning to meditate and making it daily habit is known to dramatically heighten intuition like nothing else. If you find it difficult to meditate, invest in some relaxing guided meditation CDs.

5. **Do you spend time in nature?** Go for walks in nature whenever you need a break from what you are doing. Rhythmic movements such as walking are relaxing. The color green is known to relax us. A relaxed mind is a clear mind, and a clear mind brings forth answers. You are also more apt to come up with a solution or new idea when you get away from the problem and stop focusing on it for a while.

6. **Have you become aware of signs pointing you on your way?** Give your subconscious a command to open you up to seeing the signs. Tell your subconscious that you want to be led to the next step in your journey. The signs will appear. Don't discount dreams, or things that you hear on the radio, TV, and in conversation, or read somewhere. Answers, guidance, and signs can and do come from anywhere.

7. **Have you connected with like-minded individuals?** Nothing will propel your forward faster than surrounding yourself with others walking the same path. Join an intuitive development group. Practice, practice, practice! If you are working on becoming a better writer, join a writer's group; if you are starting your own business, join a group for entrepreneurs. Place yourself in the likeliest place to get the answers and guidance you need on your journey. Be open, and they will come.

8. **Are you reading to expand your knowledge and open your mind to what your purpose might be?** Great ideas will inspire you and help you to evolve. To evolve is simply to expand your consciousness. As you become more conscious, you will be open to many more opportunities you would not have seen in the past. Read non-fiction books, such as self-development books or manuals in your field, and other topics. Don't discount biographies, or fiction either; some of the greatest innovations came from science fiction.

9. **Are you making time for fun?** Let your enthusiasm, joy and special gifts be a compass for the direction you take in life. When you are enthused about what you are doing and feel joyful, you become magnetic to others and attract many fortunate coincidences and helpful people. The brooding and unhappy mind will not hear intuitive guidance, but a happy joyful mind will. Take the time to plan outings to places of interest to you. Make sure you nourish your soul with fun joyful experiences often.

Chapter Three
Getting to Know Your Intuition

"All great men are gifted with intuition.
They know without reasoning or analysis,
what they need to know."

— Alexis Carrel

Developing your intuition has many practical uses

We have this ability because it is meant for us to use, to help us live better lives. It is one of the primary senses for ensuring our safety, too. For example, isn't it useful to suddenly feel that you should take a different route to work, only to find out later that there was a bridge collapse? Yes, absolutely.

Just think how much information you would receive if you chose to develop your intuition and become conscious of all these cues and bits of information all the time? Becoming aware of and then using the information coming through all the time might just put you in the category of genius.

A **genius** is "someone who shows extraordinary intellectual ability, creativity, or originality, typically to a degree that is associated with the achievement of unprecedented insight."[1]

This certainly sounds like someone using intuitive insight to me.

Intuitive hunches can put you in the category of genius and they can also play an important part in your daily life as well.

For example, one practical benefit in business is that you will be able to sniff out a serious customer from someone who will just consume your time.

There are many other practical uses for intuitive guidance.

A short list of how intuition can be used in your everyday life:

1. You can tell if someone is lying or trying to manipulate you.

2. You will know if someone is a phony and just using you.

3. You will pick the right mate or life partner.

4. You will buy the right house or condo. Or you will know now is not the time to buy.

5. You will know if you should take a certain job.

6. You will know if you are going to get along with the boss at the new job.

7. You will know if you should go out on a date with a certain person.

8. You will know if you should pursue a particular career.

9. You will know if you should hire one contractor over another to do the work on your home.

10. You will know to pick the right doctor.

11. You will know if your body is developing an illness and needs early preventive medicine.

1   American Heritage Dictionary Online, s.v. "genius," accessed July 24, 2011, http://www.newworldencyclopedia.org/entry/Genius

12. You will know if you should order that expensive piece of furniture or whether you will hate how it looks in your house upon delivery.

13. You will be able to determine which clients to call on what days.

14. You will be able to pick better investments or the right financial advisor.

15. You will know the exact time to call a prospect and when they will be receptive to you.

16. You will know who is going to be of help to you and who isn't.

17. You will know who is going to buy from you versus waste your time.

18. You will know if one of your child's friends is a bad influence on him or her.

19. You will know whether you should take a certain class or study with a certain teacher.

20. You will know if this is the right time to get a pet for your family.

21. You will know if you have made the right decision about a partner in your business.

22. You will know if the product being sold on the Internet really delivers on all it promises.

23. You can get more information on anything you are worried about and address your fears.

24. You will have a sense of whether you should follow through on a surgery, or if a second opinion is needed.

25. You will know whether you should join a new networking group

by sensing in your gut whether it will produce referral business or just be a waste of your valuable time.

The usefulness of intuition is endless; I have only scratched the surface here.

Learn to go by your feelings, not your intellect

Switch off your mind. When you switch off your mind you allow the voice of your intuition to be heard. Keeping the path of communication open to your intuition is important. It takes a person who is open to hear his or her intuition. You need to release all fear to hear your intuition, completely let go, and allow yourself to go to a place within you where the intellect is no longer in charge. When you do you will begin to hear your intuitive voice.

When you stop living in your head and reconnect to your body, your intuition will come through loud and clear. You will have all kinds of signals letting you know what your intuition wants you to do. You will activate your gut and you will "turn off" your head so that Greater Intelligence can come through.

All you need to do is *listen*. When you listen you will hear it. All it takes is a little practice, desire, and intention[2] to become an expert at hearing the voice of your intuition. Once you commit to your intention—hear your intuition and heed its guidance—your next step is to begin practicing.

When you start listening to your intuition, your life will change. Everyone around you will notice that you have changed. Your authentic self will come alive, and you will be surprised at all the things you can do and now attempt to do. You will become the master of your universe and it will be very obvious to those around you. They will want to know what you did, and what your secret is. Friends who cannot tolerate the new empowered you will slowly leave your life and be replaced with new friends who support you and understand the new you. You will be around people who are not insecure with your newfound brilliance. In fact, they will also emanate a brilliance and you will band together to create your highest and best lives. You are becoming a person endowed with

---

2   Authors note: I use the word "intention" to signify making a conscious decision to achieve or focus upon an end result that will positively impact one's life.

greatness who will contribute to the world to help make it a better place.

There are no coincidences

One of the most amazing things to happen when you start developing your intuition is that meaningful coincidences begin to pop up. You will meet the right person at the right time to help you solve some sort of problem in your life. You go somewhere and start a conversation with a person who has been working on the exact information you need.

Problems are solved as if by divine intervention. You are hesitant to sign up for a workshop you have been dying to take because you are not sure if spending the money at this time is the right decision. Right before the last day to sign up for the course an envelope comes in the mail containing a check for the exact amount of money you need. It turns out that your grandmother found a forgotten savings account she had started for you when you were a child, closed it out, and sent you a check.

Or perhaps you have just made the decision to take in a roommate and you mention it to a friend saying that you plan to put an ad on a local bulletin board. Your friend tells you about someone he met the other day who is looking to share an apartment. You meet and like the person and they move in by the end of the week.

These are just a few examples of the awesome power that is backing your desires when you open to your intuition.

Why do coincidences occur?

When we create the conscious intention to begin developing our intuition, the Greater Intelligence we are already hooked into responds to our request and begins to act upon our desires.

Most of us were raised to believe that life has to be hard. You have to be "tough" and bootstrap your way up to the top. In Western cultures this is the dominant mindset. The lone, tough, individual fights and claws his or her way through every major adversity and then comes out on top. This is the archetypal story running beneath the surface of our culture. It moves through our consciousness like a river, even if we aren't aware of it.

The funny thing is, since the Universe is "impersonal" and responds to all our requests and beliefs equally without judgment, by internalizing this cultural message the Universe provides the lives of adversity we believe will "toughen" us. Then we can emerge victorious when we finally reach our goal, just like the cultural myth. No matter what our expectation is in life, the Universe complies and provides it.

When you begin to delve into intuition development and learn that you have to "trust" it and allow it to operate through you, the Universe also complies with your new belief system by providing the corresponding circumstances.

Contrary to most Western belief systems, intuition is the exact opposite of "making things happen" by forcing them. When you begin to work with your intuition you learn that rather than "conquering" life and aggressively going after what you want, the life you desire begins to come to you. It's hard to grasp, but the short answer is this: when you start looking within for answers and guidance instead of looking outside of yourself, the Universe delivers everything you need right to your door. This is how your dreams and the world will "come to you."

The more you disassemble the belief that you have to fight for what you want and realize that reality emanates from within each of us, the more the Universe will provide exactly what you need when you need it. It seems counterintuitive, but this is exactly the way the Universe works. It's almost like you have to let go and fall to find out that the Universe will always catch you.

One of the reasons the Universe responds to us so quickly when we do relinquish control is that the very act of letting go and allowing the Universe to take over diminishes inner tension. When we learn to trust to that degree, we have achieved an inner state of balance and calm. The compulsion to get out there and "make things happen" has evaporated; therefore, we are not in an emotional tug of war over how to achieve our goals. We are now in sync with our beliefs and desires. Our expectations are aligned with our beliefs. There is no more competition between them to siphon off our power to create.

Our intentions double in strength when we have achieved this high level of trust in the Universe. It's as if we have our own personal "hotline" directly to the chief architect of the Universe who takes our call at anytime, day or night. We were born to give expression to Greater Intelligence by manifesting our creativity in the physical dimension. When you allow yourself to be a channel for Greater Intelligence, rather than thinking you are the one doing everything, your creative endeavors will be of much higher quality. You are co-creating with the Universe. When you go it alone you draw from the limited source of your human brain that cannot compete with the unlimited wisdom and intelligence of the universal mind.

Intuition is easy to overlook

Intuition is a lot like sand: it's hard to grasp and easily slips through the fingers.

Intuition is very subtle, which is exactly what makes it so easy to miss and overlook. It can come as a feeling in the gut, one that tells you that something is right or wrong, or it can come as a warning and a feeling of dread. Just as frequently, it's quiet like a whisper, or the flitting of a butterfly that touches down ever so slightly in our consciousness before disappearing.

Until you start paying attention, you may not be aware of these intuitive flashes. Once you begin to notice them, it's a bit like what happens after purchasing a new car: you start seeing that model everywhere. When you put yourself on alert to be aware of these stirrings, the same thing happens; the frequency of your intuitive insights increases. After that, once you begin using your intuition to make decisions, it takes no time at all to see serendipitous events begin to appear in your life.

The serendipitous events are proof positive that you are hearing and following your intuition. When you receive this direct knowledge, you have tapped into the source that keeps the planets in their orbit and the Earth spinning on its axis. This infinite intelligence doesn't make mistakes. By plugging into it and using these intuitive insights, your life flows. All the details come together seamlessly.

Most people don't recognize or trust their intuition

The hardest part about getting started with intuition is learning to recognize the voice of intuition over that of your own thoughts and trusting what you get. Intuitive thoughts stream through the mind more rapidly than our own thoughts. Not only that, but when they do appear they are usually complete ideas. In many cases they feel as if they were down-loaded "whole" into the brain. As far as trust goes, only jumping in with both feet and following hunches enough times to know that it's real will build that trust.

The best time to start developing your intuition is now. Don't wait until you finish this book.

Five easy things you can start doing to ramp up your intuition and put it to work for you right away:

1. **Create the intention to begin noticing your intuition.** Tell your-self that you wish to become aware of your intuitive insights and that you will become aware of them.

2. **Keep a small notebook with you at all times** where you can jot down any thoughts that appear to have been downloaded whole into your mind without you generating them.

3. **Give yourself many opportunities to practice.** Before answer-ing the phone, ask yourself who it might be. When meeting with friends see if you get any impressions about what they will be wearing. You can come up with dozens of little tests like this.

4. **Make it a habit to have some quiet meditative time each day.** Quieting the mind is the most powerful way to boost your intuition.

5. **When you are faced with a decision close your eyes and clear your mind.** Ask yourself what you should do, and then stop think-ing. See what springs to mind no matter how silly it might be. It could be an image, a word, or a thought. Examine this closely. It's usually your answer.

Work on incorporating these tips into your life, and I guarantee you will see a huge rise in your intuitive insights and the number of seem-ingly miraculous coincidences that occur in your life.

Your body is a walking, talking radio receiver

Every day you receive thousands of impressions and feelings below the level of your conscious awareness from the environment and the people around you that help you to survive and navigate through daily life.

Did you know that you are receiving information constantly from your environment? Not a minute passes when you don't receive all kinds of data. The reason most of it bypasses the conscious mind is to avoid sensory overload and so that your mind will be able to fully concentrate on the task at hand. If every little piece of information that you came in contact with required the attention of your mind, you would have very little energy left to focus on what you were doing.

Most of this information is registered in the subconscious where it gets processed and either saved in our memory or dispatched as intuitive information. If it's classified as intuitive information, it is forwarded to a part of the body where it's translated into a physical feeling to get our attention or passed to the mind as an intuitive flash of insight.

Many of our intuitive hunches are communicated through our bodies as physical sensations. If you feel uncomfortable, get a knot in your stomach, your heartbeat speeds up—or you are repelled, physically drained by being around someone—this may be the body's way of alerting you to stay away from that person. Other sensations you may have are sweating, sweaty palms, a lump in your throat, butterflies in the stomach, a sense of dread and foreboding, or nervous feelings. Sometimes it is as simple as having a strong sense of liking or disliking someone upon meeting them.

We each have an energy pattern, or signature, that many people refer to as the aura. The energy extends quite a few feet from the body and mingles and merges with the energy of the people, places, and things we come in contact with each day. Places and objects retain the energy of all the people who have come into their space. As we interact with them, we are constantly receiving information directly from their energy system through the field of consciousness. This information is filtered through the subconscious and registered in the body as our "gut" feelings.

Have you ever gone somewhere and felt completely uncomfortable or nervous for no reason you could put your finger on?

Or have you ever met someone you immediately liked or disliked?

Did you ever have the sense that someone was lying to you?

These are all examples of picking up on information from the energy fields you come in contact with.

Learning to use this information is really helpful and gives you a competitive advantage in everything you set out to do. One of the greatest benefits of developing your intuition is that you receive more information about things in order to make better choices and decisions.

As you become more aware of how your intuition works, you will also begin to pick up more information from the people and places you visit.

Your body is intelligent

Our survival and safety is one of the most practical reasons why our intuition communicates with us. If we are not aware of danger because the information isn't communicated to us verbally—or we aren't reading it, hearing it, or seeing it—how are we receiving these impressions and feelings?

There are numerous other "senses" beyond the five common senses that constantly impart information to us through our bodies. You truly are a walking, talking intuitive radio receiver and transmitter. Whether or not you know it and believe it, you are intuitive!

Gut feelings and "butterflies" in the stomach

An area of your body that acts as a receiver is your gut, the area surrounding the navel.[3] Have you ever experienced the "fight or flight" response in a fearful situation? When your gut is activated you "feel" it.

The gastrointestinal system or *solar plexus* area of our body has been referred to as the "second brain."[4] Science has learned that this system shares some similarities with our brains. Our digestive tracts contain neurons and produce serotonin and dopamine just as the brain does. This is the reason why we experience much of our emotional processing in our gut. For example, have you ever experienced that "punched in the gut"

3   Authors note: The "gut" is the region on the body also referred to as the "solar plexus." It is best described as extending out from two to three inches in circumference around the belly-button.

4   Adam Hadazy, "Think Twice: How the Gut's "Second Brain" Influences Mood and Well-Being. The emerging and surprising view of how the enteric nervous system in our bellies goes far beyond just processing the food we eat," *Scientific American*, February 12, 2010. http://www.scientificamerican.com/article.cfm?id=gut-second-brain

feeling after a traumatic emotional event? That is the "second brain" registering the effects of that event.

- The solar plexus is in the area around the naval.

- This area has been associated with wisdom, personal power, and fulfillment by ancient systems of knowledge.

- "Gut feelings" or "butterflies in the stomach" are the direct result of your body receiving information and trying to get your attention to analyze this data.

Think about it: when you last had a gut feeling, wasn't it either a warning to stop or a signal to go ahead with something in your life? Is this not "wisdom" that directly affects your personal power and fulfillment?

You are intuitive and receiving intuitive impressions all the time, whether or you choose to accept it or not.

Receiving information intuitively is necessary and vital to your safety and security.

Several common ways you might be receiving information intuitively on a daily basis:

1. Did you ever answer the phone "knowing" who was calling? How did you know?

2. Were you ever aware that someone was looking at you? How did you know this?

3. Have you ever thought of someone you have not seen for a long time and then randomly run into them, or heard from them? Why did you think of them after all that time?

4. Has a thought ever suddenly "stood out" and gotten your attention? Have you heard something like an inner voice urgently saying: "Call Mom!" And, even if you ignored it and got involved in

something else, the inner voice nagged at you until you listened and called your mom?

5. Were you ever trying to solve a problem in your life, when suddenly, out of the blue, when you were no longer concentrating on it, the answer came to you and you "knew" it was right?

6. Have you ever sensed something was going to go wrong or had gone wrong? Did you have butterflies in your stomach? You weren't sure what had gone wrong, but you felt it in your gut?

7. Did you ever meet someone and take an instant liking or disliking to them? You just "felt" that you should or shouldn't associate with this person?

8. Have you ever sensed you were in danger long before it became obviously apparent? Did that fight or flight response kick in? If so, you were getting this information via the "second brain."

9. Were you ever compelled to do something, even though all the so-called "experts" tried to dissuade you? You just "felt" in your gut that it was the right thing to do, you couldn't shake it until you did it, and it turned out to be brilliant?

How many of these nine intuitive responses have you experienced? Can you see how valuable it is to receive information in ways beyond the five senses? Has it ever helped you make a decision?

Your body is always communicating with you

When we are under stress many of us feel it in our stomachs. We feel a pain, or pressure, or tightness in the gut area. This is where our body registers the message that we are under too much pressure. It wants us to relax and take it easy and to move out of the stressful situations we are in.

Stress responses are how the body processes much of the information it receives from the outside world. Many things we see with our eyes don't actually get registered in the conscious mind, but your subconscious mind registers them. If there is danger, it will flood your body with the hormone cortisol[5] in order to induce the "fight or flight" response that is needed for you to get to safety.

When cortisol is being pumped into veins, it causes your heart and breathing to speed up. The next time you are under stress, notice if you feel your heart racing. You may also notice that your breathing is shallower. These are both very common reactions to stress.

If we are around someone or involved in a task and we feel lifeless, weak, or upset, our intuition is trying to warn us that this person or situation is no good for us. If, on the other hand, we feel good around certain people, or in a certain situation, or doing a certain task energizes us and makes us feel more alive, then our intuition is waving a flag and saying, "Go!"

Our intuition uses different ways of sensing to communicate with us

Clair is the French word for "clear."

After some time of working with your intuition, you may find yourself developing heightened sensitivities, sometimes referred to as psychic abilities or extrasensory perception (ESP). When this starts happening you may well see the "clairs" kicking in.

Clairsentience—means "clear feeling." This is the ability to pick up emotions and feelings about others. You may get strong feelings that are quite specific, such as your boss is upset or in danger. You get the sense that she might have had an accident. You can't shake it and it persists. Later at the office, the boss walks in and is in a foul mood because of a fender-bender on the way to work.

Clairaudience—"Clear hearing." This will manifest as hearing a thought in your mind that stands out above your other thoughts. It seems to be "loud" in comparison. You may even think that others are hearing it but, it will be "heard" in the mind, not with your physical ear. On rare occasions it may actually be a voice coming from outside of you that only you hear. The majority of times, though, what you will hear will be your own thoughts, only one in particular seems to stand out.

---

5   New World Encyclopedia Online, s.v. "cortisol," accessed July 24, 2011 http://www.newworldencyclopedia.org/entry/Cortisol.

I have twice heard this strong male voice direct me to take very specific jobs. Both times I was in the midst of personal transition and not sure which way to turn when I received this guidance. The surprising thing was that in both instances I would not have thought to go into either of these two businesses on my own, yet both experiences ended up being very beneficial to my life and growth.

Claircognizance—"Clear knowing" occurs when you just "know" something. You have no way of knowing *how* you know, but you know. When you get this "knowing" it's quite emphatic. There is no wavering about it. It appears in your mind as a complete, fully formed idea, and not one that you would been thinking about beforehand.

Sometimes, when I meet people for the first time, I immediately "know" things about them. And sometimes I will just "know" that a person is going through a tumultuous time, or that he or she has suffered the loss of someone.

Clairvoyance—is "clear seeing." It is sometimes referred to as "remote viewing." With clairvoyance you will see something, a scene, a symbol or a person in the mind's eye. It's only visible to you. Initially, you may find that this happens during meditation when your eyes are closed, but with time it can begin happening when the eyes are open, too.

The way it began for me is that I used to "see" peoples' homes in my mind. I'd ask them if they lived in a blue house, with white shutters, for example, and they would verify that they did.

A word of caution is important here. Some of the images you will receive clairvoyantly will be symbols and not literal representations of what you are seeing. As you start to receive more symbols, it would be a good idea to keep a list of the symbols you have received and what they turned out to represent. Many times a symbol repeats itself, so knowing what it stands for in your mind would help you to make sense of it in the future.

Clairgustance—is "clear smelling." It isn't as common as the other "clairs," but it does happen. I am very aware of the smell of cigarettes once in a while, yet I don't smoke and neither does anyone in my household. The smell is a signal that my aunt, who was a smoker, is visiting me. I know she's around when I get a whiff of cigarette smoke. I've also gotten whiffs of perfume when doing readings for people and it was not from the person I was reading for (most of my readings are done by telephone). The perfume smell is usually a clue about the person I'm reading for, or the kind of perfume they wear.

Clairalience—is "clear tasting." Clairalience is the least common of the "clairs." However, it does happen from time to time. You should be aware of it in case it happens to you.

I was taking my aunt for a doctor's check-up. She had just completed a round of chemotherapy. I had a terrible metallic taste in my mouth. It tasted like I was sucking on coins picked up from the dirty floor of the New York subway. When I described it to her she confirmed the taste as similar to what she experienced after a heavy dose of chemotherapy.

Understanding the "clairs" is an important step in your growth with intuitive work. These sensing modes offer a rich source of information when getting answers for yourself or others.

Premonitions—knowledge of future events

Many people confuse premonitions and fearful daydreams. I've had people ask me about this quite a bit. You need to recognize that a premonition presents itself to you. It's not something you have been consciously worrying about. Worry is your mind going over and over the same things in a loop.

A **premonition** is suddenly downloaded whole into your awareness and it has a feeling of finality to it. You know that a premonition is real. With worry, your mind acts like a squirrel that got into the house: it jumps all over the place in a panic. A premonition is the complete opposite of that. It doesn't arise from our regular, linear, thinking mind. You just know; that is all.

A **presentiment** is when you get a sense of the future through emotion. Presentiment is similar to a premonition. You have a strong feeling of dread or nervousness but you don't know what to attribute it to. You might "feel" nervous that something is about to happen but won't know why.

With premonitions you have the details at the moment you receive this information. For example, when my father asked me to take him to the emergency room for a minor procedure two years before he died, I heard this: "And so it begins." I suddenly "knew" this would not be the last time I would bring him to the emergency room. The "knowing" was accompanied by a feeling of dread that this was the beginning of the end. Premonitions are thoughts or ideas that are complete with the details of the event.

With presentiment you won't know why you have this feeling until you learn from someone or something about the event that caused the feeling of dread or fear. A recent example of presentiment I had was where I was nervous and had butterflies in my stomach all day. I kept wondering what was going to go wrong. Later in the evening I found out I had won free tickets to a conference I planned to attend! Premonitions and presentiment can be forewarnings of both good and upsetting events to come in your life.

Strengthen your memory to become a better intuitive

With so much going on in our busy lives today, we need good memories just to keep all the details of our many appointments straight. It is believed that the amount of information that is produced in the world doubles every four years. With so much information flooding our society, retention becomes a problem.

How do you decide what is important to retain? Trying to remember everything is virtually impossible and, with what we try to retain on a daily basis alone, we are constantly hearing about people having "fuzzy thinking" and difficulty remembering things. This is due to the stress we are all under because of our extreme addiction to busyness, electronic communication devises, multitasking, and just the sheer volume of information our minds are bombarded with on a daily basis.

Our memory is also extremely important in intuitive work and development as well. The better your memory is the more details you will retain of a lightning fast intuitive flash or an image that flies through your mind. Intuitive information isn't like our thoughts. We don't produce them, so we aren't in control of when they are going to manifest. We might be on our way to the airport driving on a busy highway when a flash drops into our awareness unannounced. We are focused on driving and watching for the airport exits; we don't have the luxury of ruminating over the flash that just went by in a nanosecond.

We need to develop strong memories beforehand so that we retain the brilliance our intuition is sending us.

Easy memory-strengthening exercises

I suggest using at least one, once per week

1. The next time you are in line at the market, study the face of the person at the cash register. Quickly! See how many of the details you can get in just a few seconds. While the person rings up your order and you are bagging, don't look at the cashier and see how much of his face you can retain. When you are finished and paying the cashier look the cashier in the face and see if the picture you held in your mind was correct. How did you do?

2. Make your usual list the next time you have to run to the store to pick up a few items. I suggest starting off with those in-between grocery runs where you have no more than five to seven items to pick up. Go over the list and study it before you leave the house. Then put it in your pocket. When you get to the store do not use your list. Go through the store and pick out your items. Before you leave and get in the checkout line, review the list to be sure that you didn't forget anything. How many things did you remember? Did you forget anything?

3. While doing light housework put on your favorite pop radio station. The reason I specifically advise listening to pop is because the songs are shorter. When you find your station, begin listening. See how many songs you can remember out of the set before the next commercial. Listen to the DJ when he or she goes over the playlist before the next set starts. The reason this exercise is very good for strengthening your memory is because you are concentrating on cleaning while you are listening. It's a good simulation for the same conditions you may be under when the next hunch or flash comes up. You may not be cleaning, but will probably be engrossed in some other activity at the same time when one of these intuitive ideas touches down. This will beef up your retention.

4. When you are introduced to a new group of people, commit each of their names to memory. Look closely at each of their faces and find a feature that stands out. Keep repeating the names silently

and associating it with a feature. See the person's face in your mind as you do this. See how well you remember each of their names later on. This is an excellent exercise. How many of us are introduced to people and, as soon as they walk away, we forget their names? How embarrassing is it when we bump into them and have no idea what their name is?

It really doesn't take much to see improvement in your memory if you practice doing some of these fun exercises.

Chapter Four

Developing Your Intuition

"The intellect has little to do on the road to discovery. There comes a leap in consciousness, call it Intuition or what you will, and the solution comes to you. You don't know how or why."

— Albert Einstein

Why meditation is so important for developing your intuition

When we meditate we calm the mind and go to a deeper, more relaxed state of mind. As our mind slows the frequency of our thoughts, the brain's electrical activity slows down. This has been verified by reports that map out brain waves called electroencephalograms (EEG). EEG machines measure the electrical activity of the brain. Studies show that our brains produce varying rhythms or brain waves, according to the activities we are engaged in. When we are relaxed or meditating our brain slows down and produces "alpha waves," which have been correlated with creative thinking.

When you make meditation a habit, your intuition will increase exponentially because intuition is at peak potential in a calm mind. It is the single most important thing you can do to develop your intuition. In fact, if you do nothing else in this book, do learn to make meditation a habit. It is the gold standard for increasing your intuition as well as giving you many other benefits,[1] such as remaining calm throughout the day, reducing stress levels, and aiding your immune system, just to name a few. Studies of meditation are well documented. It is miraculous in many ways, and I highly encourage you to begin meditating.

While we are awake and going through our daily routines, our minds are producing predominantly faster wave rhythms. When we meditate or daydream or relax deeply, our mind produces alpha waves. When we produce these slower electrical brain rhythms, we are usually in a more creative and receptive state of mind and are open to more ideas and answers, as well as intuitive flashes and hunches.

The reason we want to make meditation a habit is so that we regularly spend quality time producing more alpha waves.[2] When we learn to relax, we program our minds to create a habit of slowing down to receive inspiration, guidance, and flashes of intuition. By committing to a daily practice of meditation, you are programming your mind to know that each day you wish it to slow down and allow this brilliance to come through to you. After doing this for a while, your mind will start to slow down the minute you approach the hour that you regularly meditate. It will become an ingrained habit by then. That is a good reason to meditate at approximately the same time each day.

Your mind is overstressed as it is. We tend to think way too much in our society. Even our down time is now infringed upon by all the electronic devices we are addicted to, so that we are never really giving our brain a chance to rest aside from sleeping. Studies show that most of us don't get enough sleep. So, by meditating regularly, you will gain the additional benefit of relaxation along with developing your intuition.

---

1   Mayo Clinic Staff, "Meditation: a simple, fast easy way to reduce stress," accessed July 24, 2011. http://www.mayoclinic.com/health/meditation/HQ01070.
2   Funk & Wagnalls New World Encyclopedia Online, s.v. "ELECTRO-ENCEPHALOGRAPHY," accessed July 26, 2011 EBSCO*host*

Learning to meditate

Here are the steps for learning to meditate the easy way if you are not already practicing.

1. Go somewhere in your home where you won't be disturbed. Make sure you tell your family that you need some quiet time; ensure that they cooperate. You don't want your child running in and disturbing you just when you have settled down.

2. Sit in a comfortable chair where your back can be supported and you can sit up straight. Make sure your feet are flat on the floor in front of you. You don't want to have your legs crossed.

3. Put your hands down on your thighs. You can have them palms down or palms up, whichever is more comfortable for you.

4. Start taking some deep breaths in through your nose. Hold them for a few moments, and then release through the mouth. Let your breath out slowly. This is a great way to release tension and stress. Do this at least twenty times.

5. At some point you will lose count. That is okay. Just start over at one again. By focusing on the breathing, you will naturally slow your thoughts down. You will be focused on the counting and not on thinking. By allowing the mind to slow down and stop thinking, you will be giving your brain a much needed rest from overuse. This is when you will begin to sense how relaxed and calm you are. When you are relaxed and calm intuitive guidance is much more likely to get through.

6. If you have thoughts, allow them to go through your mind. But immediately begin your breathing and counting again. After a while your brain will get the idea that this is not "thinking time" but "rest time," and the thoughts won't interrupt you so much.

You will never be able to stop thinking completely, so don't feel bad if you still have thoughts popping up. You will have moments when you are aware that you have no thoughts in your head. These are the moments that you will feel the most calm and serene.

After a while you may be able to maintain this thought-free state for longer periods. But, again, don't feel you are not doing it right or not good at meditation if you have thoughts coming in. This is natural. Even the most seasoned meditation practitioner cannot maintain a thought-free mind endlessly. Just go back and start counting your breaths again. The more you stick with this process, the more you will train your mind to slow down your thinking at these times. Repetition and practice are the keys to meditation mastery.

That is it. See how simple this was? You can start with just five or ten minutes a day, whichever you find most comfortable and convenient. If you feel inspired and have the time, you can stay in the meditative state for twenty minutes or longer. I usually meditate for a minimum of twenty minutes—longer when I have the time.

The best time to begin practicing is when you are still a bit groggy in the morning. When you are not quite wide awake, your thoughts are already slower. This will help you to get into that relaxed state of mind more easily.

Practice this first thing in the morning. I suggest not getting out of bed if you can help it. If you have to get up to use the bathroom, avoid turning on any lights. Keep your eyes half-closed so that you don't become too awake.

Sit up in your bed. It is best not to lie down with the covers over you since it is likely that you will fall asleep again. Put the pillow up behind you against your headboard and then start your breathing.

Do this for five consecutive mornings. After the fifth day you will find that you naturally begin to feel more relaxed as soon as you prop the pillows up behind you. You have now conditioned your mind to anticipate the wonderful relaxing effects of meditation.

Even if you meditate only five minutes in the beginning, the benefits will last all day.

On the sixth day you can start doing the same meditation before going to sleep at night.

1. Prop the pillows up against your headboard and follow the previous steps.
2. After the twenty breaths, just sit up for a few more moments and notice how calm and peaceful you are.
3. Put the pillows back down and put your head down and go to sleep. I guarantee you will sleep like a log.

Now you know how to do a simple meditation. The next phase is to start making both the morning and evening meditations longer. If you have only been meditating for five minutes, then go to ten minutes twice a day. Then move to fifteen minutes and then to twenty minutes. Twenty minutes two times per day is all you need. If you can't fit in twenty minutes, try at least fifteen minutes two or three times per day.

Don't be concerned if you lose track of your inhalations. This is okay. Just get back into it and count again. When you get to twenty without losing count you can stop counting. Just continue to breathe in through the nose and out through the mouth. At this point you will feel very relaxed. Continue to maintain this very relaxed state for up to twenty minutes, twice a day. If you start thinking, go back to counting your breaths again. When you get to twenty breaths without losing count you can stop and enjoy the calming effects again.

This is a basic beginner's meditation. There is much more to learn about meditation, and many other methods, but most meditation techniques begin with the focusing on the breath, so be sure to master this first.

After a while you will find that, when you are in this state, answers to problems you have been grappling with will arise. You will get a clear sense of what to do next or how to address a problem. You may even begin to have some moments of greater clarity about your life. Your true purpose may reveal itself.

Let go of bad habits

Bad habits begin to fall off with regular meditation because we are now returning to a calmer state of using our minds. We are not swinging wildly with each emotion that surfaces. We are able to observe the emotion but not let it take hold of us and bat us about like a wind sock. When we have this calm way of approaching our day, we will have less drama in our lives and, consequently, less stress.

Less stress in our daily lives allows us to return to our natural state of calm. We can more easily let go of addictive habits when our stress levels drop. This is the time to join Weight Watchers® or get that nicotine patch. You will be amazed at what you can accomplish when you allow your racing mind to return to its natural state of calm.

The benefits of meditation are well documented.[3] It takes only twenty cumulative hours of meditation to make physical changes to the brain's neural pathways. We can reprogram ourselves completely over just a few weeks with meditation.

If you were quick to anger, you may begin noticing you are calmer and more able to deal with your emotions than you were previously. You may have also begun to observe your emotions and realize you can choose not to react to them. Meditation improves your immune system by lowering stress, too. Meditation is also known to help students learn more easily.

Meditation for improving intuition

Hopefully, you have already begun meditating for twenty minutes, twice a day. It should be feeling natural to you now. You should be looking forward to meditation and seeing yourself changing.

You may also be noticing that you have many more intuitive flashes than you had in the past. You suddenly get a gut feeling about something or a "knowingness" about what to do. These are some of the benefits of meditating.

Guided meditation to develop your intuition

Now you are ready to begin developing your intuition with a guided meditation exercise.

---

3   Science Daily Staff, "Mindfulness Meditation Training Changes Brain Structure in Eight Weeks" *Science Daily*, January 21, 2011. http://www.science-daily.com/releases/2011/01/110121144007.htm.

- Get into your comfortable position and do your breathing. When you get to that calm place after your twenty breaths you are ready to do the following exercises. It is fine if you feel you are completely relaxed after counting less than twenty breaths. You may not need to count to twenty breaths once you have been practicing for a while. That is okay. You are making progress. You are becoming accustomed to meditating and you don't need that "crutch" anymore. You don't have to be so regimented once you reach that point. If you start to have a lot of thoughts going through the mind again, get back to your counting of breaths.

- Once you feel you are in a state of deep relaxation, see yourself in your mind's eye in a peaceful environment—a beach, lake, or whatever represents a calm place for you. See yourself at this place. Feel the warm sun on your skin, and hear the sounds of nature around you. Hear the ocean or the water rushing in the stream beside you. See yourself resting on a blanket in this serene place. This is your own personal inner sanctuary that you can return to anytime you meditate.

- Now, sit there and enjoy this wonderful, peaceful environment. Ask yourself a question. Perhaps you are grappling with whether to take a certain job (Substitute any problem you are grappling with). Ask yourself how you would feel if you proceeded with taking this new job. While mulling over this question, you notice on the horizon a small plane flying in the air. It has a banner attached to it with some words written on it. It's too far away. You can't make them out just yet. As it gets closer you can read the words on the banner. What do they say?

- This should be the answer to your question pertaining to how you would feel if you took this job offer. If you don't see any words, don't feel bad. This takes practice and time. Concentrate on the feeling you got instead.

- Just stay in that place of relaxation. You will get better with practice over time. For now, try to see the plane. It is flying away from you, far into the horizon. You hear the engine slowly fade out. The sky is blue and the clouds are white and billowy. You hear the plane coming closer again. It's still far off in the distance; it hasn't moved close enough to be in your field of vision yet. It finally comes close enough to see. This time you are able to read the words on the banner flying off the tail.

- What does it say? You have your answer. Allow yourself to feel the answer. How does it feel? Do you feel good about the answer? Continue with this exercise even if you didn't see anything written on the banner.

- While keeping your eyes closed, place your hands on your abdomen to establish a connection to your inner wisdom. How do you feel? Are you okay with the answer you received? If you didn't see anything, just use an answer such as, "Yes, I have decided to take the job." Does this resonate with you? Are you suddenly scared about leaving your current job? Or do you feel a sense of relief to leave the job that you are tired of? Are you excited and energized by the idea of the new job?

Is your heart racing a bit? Are you noticing a lump in your throat? These are signs that you may not be ready to take the plunge. Sometimes we think we should do something and that it will be for our own good but, really deep down inside, we are not ready. When we are not ready, the body's reactions will tell us. We can lie to ourselves with the rational mind, but the body will register this as a lie.

How to use journaling to awaken your intuition

Journaling is a fabulous way to gently coax your intuition out of hiding. Many times we can get our feelings out on paper much easier than we can articulate them. We can write in secret, pouring our hearts out into a journal, without any fear of judgment or being made to feel ashamed.

The best time to journal is right after meditation in the mornings. Getting up an hour earlier each day in order to incorporate meditation and journaling is really worth it. It should become part of your day, just like brushing your teeth. What you are doing when you make the time to meditate and journal is showing yourself that you think you are worthy of this extra attention and special "you" time. Nurturing your inner growth with these activities also sends a clear message to your intuition that you are serious about developing an open dialogue with it. You are showing how strongly you desire to open the channels of communication between you.

Making a habit of journaling, just like you did with meditation, amplifies the intuitive voice even more. When you pour your heart out onto the page, insights will arise. You will find yourself having many aha moments when you start opening up to your journal.

In many ways journaling is like having a conversation with a counselor. The more you open up the more you have to work with and the more insights you will have. Each insight helps you understand yourself a little better and helps you to work out problems and get answers to those problems.

In the beginning you may find yourself writing more about your emotional reactions to certain problems. Over time, as you express these emotional reactions on the page and get them out of your system, you will see that your journaling will start to change. It will go from a reflection of your daily life and problems to a reflection of your inner growth and the insights you are having about life.

You will find that your intuition will begin to tune in through your journaling sessions. Invite your intuition to come through.

Each morning start your journaling with this sentence:

I invite and welcome my intuition to join me in this journaling session today. I am open to hear what you have to say.

Then just start writing. If you like you can set a timer for a half-hour. It actually works best if you write very quickly without stopping and not going back to read what you have written until afterward. If you have more time, you can forgo the timer, but setting a limit does work. It means you have to push a lot out of you within a short amount of time. Giving yourself more time doesn't always mean you will get better results. Working with a journal is about going deep and bringing up the hidden treasure from the depths of your soul.

Stick to journaling and make sure to allow time in your day for this important communication with your intuition.

Letting your higher intelligence "write" through you

This is called direct writing. It is "direct" because you are tapping into Greater Intelligence by writing with your non-dominant hand.

Direct writing is a method that allows you to bypass the rational thinking mind. Using your non-dominant hand connects you to the right brain hemisphere, which is the side of the brain that our intuition communicates through. We call it direct writing because it links you directly with your creative and intuitive mind.

Take a pad of paper and write your question across the top of it with your dominant, writing hand.

- Now take your pen in the opposite hand and rewrite the question. Now allow the non-dominant hand to start writing.
- Try not to "think" about what the hand is writing. Allow higher intelligence to give you the answer. It may feel awkward at first, but the more you do it the easier it will become. You can even turn away from the writing so that you cannot see what is being written.
- After the writing has stopped, read your answers. You will know it's time to stop when you feel the energy drop. You will be very surprised at what has come out.

Accessing intuitive guidance through dreams

One of the best times for our intuition to speak to us is through our dreams. You can accomplish this easily. You are already trained on how to go to sleep and you have already had lots of dreams. The only thing you need to do differently is to make sure you have a pad and pencil on your night table to write down the dream once you wake up.

Sit up in bed and do your evening meditation. Give yourself a directive that you are going to have a dream that answers a question you have or that solves a problem you have been dealing with. Tell yourself you will absolutely remember it.

Go directly to sleep afterward. Write your dream down immediately when you wake up in the morning. Do not do anything else—don't get out of bed, don't go to the bathroom and, in fact, don't move a muscle until you have the dream firmly planted on your pad. If you move, you are guaranteed to forget this dream.

You don't have to spend an hour writing down your dream. Just jot down the main points so that you won't forget it. When you return, read what you have written. Now go into your morning meditation. Review the dream. How does it apply to your problem? Were you able to analyze it? Does it shed light on your problem? How will you apply the wisdom of the dream to your life?

Dreams are an easy way to gain intuitive guidance, which makes it great for beginners. Recalling your dreams will dramatically increase your intuition, too. Why? Because Greater Intelligence will see that you are mining your dreams for answers, so more answers will be sent via this method of communication. The more you want help, the more Greater Intelligence will send help your way.

Greater Intelligence is always pressing up against us looking for ways to become involved in our lives. When we start asking for its help, it's as if we have given Greater Intelligence an open door through which to walk right into our lives. So, go ahead: invite Greater Intelligence into your life. You will be glad you did.

We have many kinds of dreams

Some dreams contain intuitive guidance, and some are just crazy pieces of the day's events. Precognitive dreams foretell future events. Some dreams we have are vivid encounters with departed loved ones, and others are recollections of out-of-body experiences. Others offer intuitive guidance to solve problems and answer questions about issues we are facing in our lives.

Your intuitive dreams act as a gauge to show you whether you are on the right track in your life. Your intuition has a very practical purpose and is there to help you make the right choices, keep you safe, and act as a warning system or navigation system in your life.

Solutions come while you sleep

The most rewarding dreams are the problem solvers, simply because they are the most practical in everyday life. Problem solving dreams not only give you answers and guidance, but can also validate an answer or direction you are not totally sure about taking.

Intuitive guidance, at its best, gives us more information and answers so that we live better, more fulfilling lives. Getting answers to problems is the main reason for learning to remember your dreams.

For example, before I quit my high-stress job I had this dream:

I was in the car driving to a client meeting. I spotted my aunt, who had passed away, on the sidewalk talking with someone. She saw me and smiled and waved me over. I gave her a signal to wait for me and shouted through the open window that I would be back. She looked very disappointed. I was aware that she was no longer living, and that she'd come back for a special visit with me. I was really torn knowing I'd rather be with her than going to this meeting. When I returned after my meeting, she was no longer there.

My dream was telling me that I was letting life pass me by. I wasn't doing what was in my heart, but only what I thought I was "supposed" to do. Soon after having this dream, I made up my mind to quit my job.

Why some people remember dreams, and others don't

When we wake up and remember we have had a crazy dream but then jump out of bed to get ready for work and forget the dream, we are sending a message that says, "I'm not interested in this information."

People who remember their dreams take time to think about them. They are interested, even if they might not understand the meaning of the dream. The message they send to the brain is, "I like remembering my dreams; send more, please!"

To start benefiting from your intuitive wisdom the easy way, program yourself to remember your dreams.

You can train yourself to remember your dreams in as little as a few nights. Once you do you will never need to worry about hearing your intuition again.

Famous Dreams

Elias Howe was the inventor of the sewing machine. He was having trouble finding the right way to thread the needle on the sewing machine. One night he had a dream about being captured by some native hunters who approached him holding spears. He noticed that their spears had holes at the bottom in the point. He woke up and immediately knew that he had gotten the answer to his problem with the sewing machine.[4] He changed the design, put the hole at the other end of the needle, and it worked!

President Abraham Lincoln had a dream shortly before his death where he heard sobbing in the White House. When he found the room where the cries were coming from, he asked what had happened. One of the mourners told him that the president had died. His dream is a famous example of a precognitive dream.[5]

Can you imagine being able to go to Greater Intelligence and asking for the answers you need? This is what you can do when you learn how to use your intuition. You can actually request help. You will learn how to do that so you don't have to wait for a random dream. You can ask whenever the problem arises and have the answer appear at will. This is the beauty of developing your intuition.

How to tell the difference between a precognitive dream and an intuitive guidance dream:

1. **A precognitive dream feels very real.** Many times you will even be aware that you are having a dream. Awareness in the dream of having a dream is called lucid dreaming.

2. **You can't forget a precognitive dream.** It's haunting and holds

---

4   Transcript of "What Are Dreams," aired on PBS November 24, 2009, *Nova*, http://www.pbs.org/wgbh/nova/body/what-are-dreams.html
5   Encyclopedia.com, "The Assassination of Abraham Lincoln," accessed July 24, 2011, http://www.encyclopedia.com/video/6qAeFjCscRY-assassination-of-abraham-lincoln.aspx
_____Daniel Harman, "Abraham Lincoln's Last Dreams," *American History Suite 101*, June 2, 2010, http://www.suite101.com/content/abraham-lincolns-last-dreams-a243976

your attention for days or weeks afterward.

3. **With a precognitive dream you will just know that it's going to be so.** No matter what you say to yourself to rationalize it, you know it's true. You can't shake the feeling of knowing.

4. **Intuitive dreams have an aha quality.** It's more of a Eureka! moment. You see the error of your ways, or get an answer to a question or situation you have been dealing with in your life.

5. **You are not aware that you are dreaming.** An intuitive dream feels like a regular dream, but with a clearly discernible message.

Keeping a dream log

The next step to access your intuitive wisdom is to keep a dream log or journal. You can record your dreams in a separate book or use the same journal you are already using. Writing down your dreams is important for two reasons.

First, by recording your dreams, you are telling your mind that it is important to you to remember them. This alone will help you to recall more of your dreams in the morning. When your mind knows that you want to do this, it will comply by making it easier and easier to remember your dreams.

Second, you want to keep a record of your dreams to be able to go back and see if you are receiving precognitive information through your dreams. Precognitive dreams give us information about the future. We may get insight into what is going to happen to us, people close to us, or about world events. Many intuitive people have precognitive dreams, even before they begin working on developing their intuition. It's one of the signs that we are all intuitive already!

When I was eleven years old I had a dream I have never forgotten about an earthquake in Japan. I was in the middle of a town square, that I just "knew" was in Japan. I was on a tricycle when the ground started to shake and all the buildings started toppling over. I remember feeling so scared because it felt so real. Then there was huge flood and I found I was trying to "peddle" my way out of the flood on my little tricycle! It has stayed with me all these years just as clear as could be to this day. When the tragic earthquake took place in Japan in March 2011, I felt that the dream I had when I was a young girl was related to this event.

Most precognitive dreams don't take years to manifest like this, although they can because time is the hardest element to predict. My mother had a dream when she was nine years old, right before World War II started, where she saw Christ appear in the sky. He said there would be great sadness and sorrow in the world soon. It really scared her at the time, and she vividly remembers it to this day. She remembers that Christ seemed to be surrounded by flames. The war began just a few months later.

When you record your dreams, you also get to analyze them in more detail if they are dreams offering intuitive guidance. When you receive this guidance, you will want to write down the feelings associated with the dream and how you think it applies to your life. I don't recommend using one of those dream interpretation books. Understanding the language of your dreams is highly personal. One symbol can mean different things to different people. You should go review the dream and then see how you feel. Compare the action in the dream to what you are going through and feeling presently in your life.

Different types of dreams: inner guidance dreams and precognitive dreams

We dream many times per night. Some dreams may not mean a thing. But I feel that, if you remember the dream, then it must mean something. You owe it to yourself to look at it closely.

When you have a precognitive dream you will know it. It will stay with you in detail for years. A precognitive dream can be literal like my dream about the Japan earthquake. It can be a dream of presentiment, meaning it includes a lot of emotions that may not make sense until after the event occurs, like the dream my mother had about World War II. In my mother's presentiment dream, she was scared and thought something awful was about to happen, but she didn't know what. Her dream didn't include any battle scenes so she had no idea it was about war, although she was scared that something was about to happen.

The difference between a precognitive dream and one where you receive intuitive guidance is that the dream offering guidance doesn't usually include knowledge of future events. For the most part, dreams offering guidance address issues we are having in the present.

I recently had a dream that my home was almost washed away by a mudslide. In the dream I lived in a townhouse (I don't in real life) that was up on a huge cliff overlooking the banks of a river. Just before the mudslide came, I scrambled up the stairs of the huge cliff and, along the way, found a knapsack on one of the stairs. When I got up to the top, I opened the knapsack and saw that it contained disaster supplies and candy. I knew I had been "saved." Luckily, my house wasn't washed away as the mudslide traveled along the banks of the river below my home.

When I wrote the dream down and began to analyze it, I realized that I was having a lot of anxiety about my living situation. I was not completely comfortable in the place where I was living and felt there was a threat that might cause me to have to vacate my house. But the knapsack told me that, even if I did have to move again, I would be fine. I had the tools to take care of myself in the knapsack. The dream was very helpful.

I can't stress enough how important it is to get your dreams down in a dream log. When you start doing intuitive work you want to be able to know and clearly understand what your current issues are.

Let's say you have a question about your daughter that you want some intuitive guidance on but, at the same time, you are dealing with some financial difficulties. You are trying to keep your head above water but you are still very worried about the future. You sit down to meditate and get some advice about how to handle your daughter's situation but the whole time your mind keeps drifting back to the financial situation you are in. If you don't deal with that situation, it will prevent you from getting the advice you seek for your daughter. So, emptying your mind in the morning and getting advice and support through a dream about your financial difficulties is not only good for your mental health but good for intuitive development. Unless you deal with the most pressing of your problems first, your intuition may elude you on the other matters you request guidance for.

When I had my dream about my living conditions, it really calmed me down to know that no matter what happened, I had the "tools" to deal with it and I would always be safe. This cleared my mind and allowed me to work on other things that needed my attention without any free-floating anxiety interfering.

Remembering your dreams

Here are the basics on how you can begin remembering your dreams to take advantage of your inner wisdom:

1. **Be prepared.** Make sure you have a pad and pen on your bedside table.

2. **Set the alarm.** Wake up a half-hour earlier to have time to mull over your dream.

3. **Create your intention.** Make up your mind to have a dream and recall it. Spend a few minutes before drifting off telling yourself that you want to have a dream, that you will have a dream, and that you will readily and easily remember it.

4. **Hold onto the images.** When you wake up do not open your eyes right away and do not move. Just lay still to allow the dream to stay on the surface of your mind.

5. **Reduce disturbances.** Do not allow pets to distract you when you wake or, better yet, keep them out of the bedroom so they don't wake you up.

6. **Jot down the details.** After retaining some of the pertinent details, write them down on your pad before they get a chance to sink back down to the depths of the subconscious. The more you work with your dreams the easier it will become to decipher them.

7. **Silence helps us recall dreams.** Don't turn on the radio, TV, or talk right after waking up. After jotting down a few details, silence allows further dream fragments to bubble up to the surface of our awareness. The best thing to do after writing down your dream is your morning meditation. Many times further dream fragments will come to mind when you meditate directly afterward.

Getting up at night makes it more difficult to remember dreams. Try to limit drinking liquids prior to going to bed. When you awaken in the midst of a dream, the movement of having to get out of bed right away grabs dreams from your mind; they are lost forever.

Follow these simple steps and after a few nights and you will find that you easily remember your dreams in the morning.

Working with muscle testing

Our body registers all kinds of information and we can decode it by using muscle testing. Muscle testing, which is also known as applied kinesiology,[6] is a method of getting information directly from the intelligence running our bodies. The source of this intelligence is Greater Intelligence. We use applied kinesiology to obtain answers by observing the response of the muscles. When using the muscles' responses for answers, we are able to bypass the logical mind, which could influence the answer to be more "logical" rather than true. We gain a truer answer by going directly to our innate intelligence.

There are numerous forms of muscle testing. One easy way to get answers through muscle testing is to work with a pendulum.

Working with a pendulum

A pendulum is a tool that shows you how your muscles are reacting to a question you asked. You can either buy one or make your own.

Here are the directions for making a pendulum:

1. Get a piece of sturdy string. Don't use sewing thread; it's too flimsy.

2. Measure the length of your wrist to your elbow. Cut your string about two inches longer.

3. Find a key or ring that you are not using and tie it onto the end of the string.

---

6   Applied Kinesiology.com, "What is AK?" accessed July 25, 2011. http://www.appliedkinesiology.com/

4. Put a nice little knot at the top of the string to help you hold it better.

5. When you tie the key to the string you should be able to hold it between your fingers. With your elbow on a flat surface and arm up, have the pendulum hang no more than a few inches from the table top.

Now ask yourself this question:

"Is my name_____ (insert your name)?"

Watch which way the pendulum moves. It may take a few moments for the key to start moving, but it will. When it starts moving take note of the type of movement.

Is it circular? Which way? Clockwise or counterclockwise?

Is it swaying from side to side? Is it swaying across in front of you horizontally or is it swaying up and down?

Whatever way the pendulum sways, know that you have established a dialogue with your body's intelligence and that this is the way the affirmative is presented. All "yes" answers from now on when using the pendulum will be shown to you using this movement.

Now ask yourself a question you know has a negative answer, such as, "Is my birthday _____ (insert an incorrect birthday)?"

Now watch which way the pendulum moves. This will be the negative response from now on when you are working with the pendulum.

Next, you must establish a way for the pendulum to show you when there is no answer yet, meaning that, at this time, this is either not for you to know or that, right now, there is no answer.

Hold the pendulum up in the manner described earlier. Tell yourself the pendulum will now show you what "No answer at this time" looks like. Wait. The pendulum will start moving. It should be in a different direction than any of the previous two responses. If for any reason you don't get a different answer, repeat this part. If the answer is still the same as one of the earlier responses, you can go back and do this entire exercise again to establish your patterns.

Now you have a way to "see" your body's intelligence at work. Now you can clearly see that all information is filtered through the body before it gets to your head, where your mind can play tricks on you. The information your body receives is pure and genuine. It hasn't been distorted by the rational mind. Using a pendulum is a good way to start tapping into your intuition.

Using the sway test

Another fun way to work with your body's intelligence or kinesiology is to use the sway test:

- Take off your shoes and move all the furniture out of the way in the room you are testing in. When you are ready and in your stocking-feet, ask yourself a question.
- If you sway forward the answer is positive, or yes. If you feel your body begins to sway backward, the answer is negative, or no.

Be sure to move the furniture out of the way so that you don't lose your balance and hurt yourself. You don't need to allow your body to sway too much. Just a hint of which direction you are moving is enough. Don't allow yourself to fall, if you can help it.

Another way of muscle testing requires another person to help you

Hold out your dominant arm so that it is parallel to your shoulder. Have the other person working with you ask you a question. Repeat the question. While you are repeating the question, the person working with you should try to push down your arm. You don't need to have the person put their entire body weight into it, though. What they are testing for is your resistance. If your arm offers good resistance to the pressure from being pushed on by your friend, then that is enough to register a positive answer or a yes.

If they are able to move your arm down, or it's loose and wiggly or wobbles easily, that would show the negative, or a no answer.

The reason your muscles react this way is because a negative or untruth takes power away from us while the positive energizes and strengthens us. It's quite simple, but amazing.

The amazing thing about our bodies is that they are receiving so much more information than we are aware of on a daily basis.

How to fire up your intuition

The best way to jump-start intuition is by making a series of snap decisions quickly every day and then taking action. I don't mean big decisions: give yourself little goals at first. One goal may be to make small decisions using your intuition. You don't want to have too much at stake. Choose decisions where it is okay to be wrong.

You are not going to decide from day one to use your intuition to pick stocks and possibly lose your entire life savings. I'm referring to small things: like when you are driving somewhere, check in with your gut to see whether you might be better off going a different way to avoid traffic. Trust the answer you get, and then do it.

Taking action on your intuitive hunches and gut feelings will get you up and running quickly. It will also help you develop a frame of reference for how your intuition feels and appears to you when it's operating.

This is one of the most important benefits of taking action early on. By developing an understanding of how your own intuition operates you will build a significant amount of trust and confidence in it much more quickly than someone who reads this book and then just waits for a time when he or she needs to tap into intuition to help make a decision.

It's part of the same principle of "use it or lose it." Use your intuition and take action immediately to start building your intuitive muscle. Another reason to take action quickly on small decisions is that you will be able to measure your rate of success easily and immediately as well.

In the example I gave earlier of taking a different route to get somewhere, you will know immediately whether or not you were right about the route you took. You may hear a traffic report after you have chosen your route informing you of a traffic jam on the route you had avoided. If you were right it will build your confidence. You will also be able to refer back to the moment you made the decision to see what you were feeling at that time, so that you have that as a point of reference for future intuitive decisions.

You should try making these snap decisions at least three of four times a day to jump-start your intuition.

Suggestions for small snap decisions you can make during the day:

1. When is the best time to go to the post office today? When will it be the least crowded: 11 a.m. or 2 p.m.? (you can substitute any hours you like)

2. What day is the best day to go shopping for that new outfit I need—when I'll walk in and see the perfect item and get in and out of the store quickly? Is it today or tomorrow?

3. Can I leave the lawn furniture out tonight or is it going to rain? (Obviously, you should not have listened to the weather forecast first. You can afterward, though; if it is going to rain, run quickly to put the patio furniture away!)

4. What should I cook for dinner tonight that my spouse will come home and say he or she was exactly in the mood for?

5. Should I go for an oil change on the car today or tomorrow? What day will the dealership be able to service my car the quickest?

You can come up with your own, but obviously you get the idea. These are small chores that won't negatively impact your life if you are wrong. Start incorporating little challenges to your intuition into your day and watch your abilities grow each day.

Keeping an intuition log

One of the things that will help you when you are making your small decisions each day is to keep a small notebook with you at all times. This is different than keeping a journal, although you can mix this in with your journal if you like.

I recommend using a different notebook, as most personal journals are rather large and will not easily stuff into a pocket or purse. (If you like, you can later incorporate these experiences into your journal.) Also, when we write in our journals, they contain a lot of sensitive information that you wouldn't necessarily want anyone else to see, even by accident. By toting around our journals we take a chance that someone might see it, or that we might be uncomfortable pulling them out in front of others, since it's a much larger book and more conspicuous. Chances are if we feel inhibited about pulling out the journal, we are going to forget to record something that happened intuitively; it's best to use a small, pocket-sized notebook.

When you get a minute, write down the snap intuitive decision you made and the outcome. Also write down how you received the intuitive information. Did you feel it in your gut? Did you just "know"? Did you hear one of your thoughts? Did a picture form in your mind? Remember, there is no right way.

Keeping this log will really help cement the relationship you have with your intuition. The Universe will also know that you are really serious about developing your intuition, too. But, the most important reason for doing it is so you can see and feel how intuitive information comes through to you.

Developing Your Intuition

Baby steps do eventually lead to big strides; this is where practice comes in. Of course, for some people, intuition might open up all at once like releasing a floodgate; for most people reconnecting to intuition isn't an overnight thing. You need to have a few experiences before you get the hang of it just like anything else. What you do is practice over and over, each time remembering what it felt like.

For example, do you remember when you met your future spouse for the first time and you "knew" that you were going to marry him or her? Can you recall when you walked into your current home after looking at homes for weeks and you just "knew" that this was the one you were going to rent or buy? Think back on some other moments like that in your life and you will have pretty good idea of what your intuition feels like when it happens the next time.

Trust in what you get no matter how odd it seems at first. Don't be afraid or worry about being wrong; that is one of the things that can kill budding intuitive abilities. Intuition isn't logical; the first time something comes up that seems illogical to you, you will want to scrap it right away. But that is precisely the thing that will turn out to be right. Intuition and logic cannot exist in the mind at the same time. You have to get rid of the need to be logical if you really intend to follow your intuition.

Here's an example of how something irrational turned out to be right

I was interviewing by phone for a job as an online psychic. The woman asked me to give her a reading right then and there as part of the interview. I began getting images about what she looked like, the room she was speaking to me from and what it looked like, the home she lived in and the views from it, as well as an insurance matter she was dealing with. Then I described her children, grandchildren, and her mother who was deceased. All of the information was correct.

The next two images that came though were very strange. I saw a man wearing a cowboy hat on a green tractor and piles of hay around him; in the background there were livestock. I felt that this was her husband and that she had been widowed. I also felt strongly that she was involved in organic farming and supplying organic food to restaurants. She told me that she was widowed, but I was not correct about the farm. She hired me anyway.

A few weeks later I was speaking to her and she told me that years ago, before her husband died, they had owned a hog ranch and supplied all the local restaurants with pork. I reminded her about the reading but she said my description had not made sense to her then; it was so long ago she had forgotten!

This is an example of how our intuition tries to encode the information into a picture to convey the information to us. I didn't connect the dots of the cowboy hat, the hay, and the livestock. All I did was focus in on the tractor because it seemed "logical." Had I tried to understand the other symbols I might have said they raised livestock instead of farmed and she might have realized what I was talking about.

Go by your feelings, not logic

Logic will tell you to go to the store by the shortest route, but the nagging feeling you get from your intuition will be telling you to take the long way when you are in a hurry. You ignore your intuition and get sidetracked in a huge traffic jam so that it takes you twice as long to get to the store. Had you listened to your intuition, you would have been there and back already. Learn to respect your intuition no matter how odd it may seem at the time.

Chapter Five

Cracking the Intuition Code

"Intuition is a spiritual faculty and does not explain, but simply points the way."

—Florence Scovel Shinn

Learning the language of intuition

Intuition has its own language. The best way to describe this language is to say that intuition communicates through feelings. A feeling will come over you, and you will immediately be able to "translate" it into a "knowing" about something. This "knowing" will contain the idea in its entirety. This is because intuition is completely different from linear thinking. You might be better off thinking of it as being similar to a hologram.

If you have seen a hologram on a credit card, you will know that it appears to be three dimensional and whole, even though the credit card is flat and two dimensional. This is the same with intuitive ideas, which are downloaded "whole" into the brain. Intuitive insights contain the complete, fully fleshed-out idea instantaneously, whereas regular thoughts are linear and follow a sequence; there is a beginning thought that leads to another and another in our thought process to arrive at the answers. Intuition is direct knowledge or wisdom that cannot be explained or arrived at through linear thinking. It simply arrives!

Once you learn the different ways intuition communicates, you will be able to decode the messages you get. There are primarily five ways[1] that intuition comes through most often, and they fall under the categories below. After working with the categories in Dr. Emory's *Intuition Workbook* for a number of years, I modified them to correspond to what I've learned through my own experience with intuition. Familiarize yourself with these five and you will soon be cracking the intuition code.

Learning to speak "intuition"

1. **Physically.** You get a gut feeling. The feeling in your gut can be fearful, nervous, anxious, cautious, hesitant, or just a feeling that something is about to happen, yet you don't know what. When the "incident" you had a gut feeling about happens—the feeling subsides. I've also experienced actual physical reactions along with feeling anxious or nervous, such as a constriction in the chest or throat, a feeling of nausea and bouts of yawning.

2. **Mentally.** It feels as though a fully formed idea has touched down out of nowhere into your mind. After your receive this "fully formed idea," it becomes a nagging thought that won't go away. And sometimes it's when you know that you know something, but you can't explain how or why you know it. It can also come as a flash of insight or can take the form of an image or symbol in the mind's eye.

3. **Empathically.** You can also pick up on the emotions of others and feeling that emotion yourself. It can also be feeling the pain others experience in your own body. It can also come in the form of taking an immediate liking or disliking to a person. It's an instinct

---

1   Emory Ph.D., Marcia, *Intuition Workbook: An Expert's Guide to Unlocking the Wisdom of Your Subconscious Mind* (Englewood Cliffs: Prentiss Hall, 1994) p. 13.

you have about someone. You may also pick up feelings from your pets.

4. **Signs and affirmations.** Things like missing the train to work only to find out later that there was a huge problem with the railways and all the trains stopped running for hours. Or considering a job change with a company you are nervous about and then seeing an article on the front page of the paper or hearing a report about them on the radio stating that this company is rated one of the top companies to work for.

5. **Hearing a distinctive thought or a voice.** This may occur less frequently, but it does happen. You have been trying to solve a problem and thinking about it over and over. Suddenly, you hear a voice that seems loud enough to have been heard by others but, judging from their faces, no one heard it but you. It came from within your mind, but it wasn't in your own voice and it had the exact answer you had been searching for, such as, "Go for that job!"

Start paying attention and looking for these encoded messages; believe me, you are getting them! You are just not aware until you focus and tune in. It may also be your own thought, but one that stands out from the other thoughts you have and is in your own voice.

How to find which of the five areas your intuition seems to favor

I suggest keeping detailed notes on all your intuitive experiences for at least one month—longer is better. Categorize every occurrence under one of the five channels when you are recording it. At the end of the month, you should see a pattern starting to emerge. Most likely you will have at least two channels that are used more than any other. Once you understand how your intuition communicates with you, begin to focus on those two channels.

If your intuition uses your body to communicate, start paying more attention to your physical reactions to things. If you realize you pick up on the emotions of others, try focusing on your own feelings to see if they are truly yours or belong to someone else. If you receive images visually, start closing your eyes after asking questions to see what you "see." If you notice that you receive answers as thoughts placed in your mind or you hear a voice, be sure to close your eyes and quiet your mind in order to listen when you are trying to receive guidance. If your intuition uses signs, ask for signs to guide you and you will get them.

The more you pay attention and tune in, the more messages your intuition will start sending you.

After keeping notes for three weeks to a month, you will see which channel your intuition favors. The good thing about this is that you can choose to heighten your abilities even further in the channels you seem to favor or you can decide you want to develop another area of your intuition that might be underdeveloped.

The more you work with your intuition overall, the more your sensing abilities will open up across the board. Many people begin their journey by realizing they are intuitive, with practice they become psychic. All their channels begin to work.

For example, some people get strong feelings about others and over time start to "see" things and "hear" things while around other people. What happens is that their other channels of communication open up and begin contributing information.

Using intuition to solve real-life problems

Working with your intuition is practical. Once you have learned to "speak intuition" you can get answers to any problem you are dealing with in life. The rest of this chapter contains several exercises to help you get answers for specific problems you might be facing. The exercises cover every aspect of our lives, from career and finances to health and relationships.

You can use them all, one by one, or go directly to the area you need help with first.

Career and finance

Use this exercise to uncover the best way to bolster your income immediately, decide whether you should invest in a certain stock, go into a certain business, or take a certain job. It can be used to uncover new opportunities such as new jobs, professions, or businesses.

Many people feel uncomfortable dealing with their personal finances. It's hard to concentrate on any other problems in your life if you are dealing with financial difficulties. In that case, the best thing to do is address them intuitively to get some advice on how to deal with them and get some relief.

Formulate a question in your mind that you need guidance on in this area before you go into your meditation.

For example, say you are looking for a new job. Your question might be, "What information would be most helpful to me now to put me on the right road to finding my perfect work?"

Or, if you are having financial problems, you might ask, "What can I do to get some relief right now from the financial problems I'm experiencing?"

Visualization exercise for career and finance

- Go into your meditative state. After you are feeling relaxed and resting peacefully at your sanctuary, take a few deep cleansing breaths and go deeper. See and feel yourself sitting there and hear the soothing sounds of nature around you.

- Out of the corner of your eye you spy a hooded figure wearing long robes. Something urges you to follow this person.

- You get up and begin following, being careful to stay back quite a distance so that he won't be aware of your presence. As you follow the hooded figure, he enters a dark cave that is ahead on the side of a hill.

- You enter the cave, which is lit by a few candles at the front. It's a long, narrow cave and has the feel of a tunnel. Up ahead you make out the hooded person going through a door on the left side at the front of the cave. You catch up and follow him through the door.

- As you go through the door, you enter brilliant sunlight. It blinds you at first, and you lose track of the hooded figure for a moment. Then you see that he is up ahead.

- He is walking down a clearing in a wooded thicket. You follow him past bushes and trees and then watch as he disappears. You pick up speed and realize that he has come to a cliff and, at first, it appears that he has walked off of it.

- You get to the edge of the cliff and see some stairs and a hand rail. You walk down the stairs to a plaza. The hooded figure is sitting on a stone bench. Then this individual looks right at you.

- The individual beckons you over and invites you to sit down. The wise being gives you his name and tells you that he knows you are in need of financial guidance and that if you give him permission, he has some advice to share with you.

- You give your permission and the guide begins to instruct you on what you can do to help your situation. Don't be surprised if the wise being tells you to call a certain person, or to go to a certain place at a certain time; just be sure to remember what he tells you.

- You have a long discussion with this guide and ask many questions, which the wise being has all the answers to. When your questions have been answered to your satisfaction you thank the wise guide. He tells you that you can return to this place anytime you need any financial guidance and he will be there waiting for you. You thank the wise being, get up, and return to your sanctuary, following the same route you took to get there.

You now feel at ease and at peace. You now have the information you need to proceed to deal with the situation at hand. After you return to your sanctuary, sit down and review what the guide told you to do and commit it to memory. Come out of your meditation. Record this session in your journal, and be sure to follow the advice this guide so lovingly gave you.

Relationships

Relationships are problematic for many people. You may be in a romantic relationship that is difficult or going through problems, or you may be having difficulties with a child, parent, friend, business partner, or colleague. No matter how much success we experience in any other area of our life, if our relationships are difficult we will not operate at full capacity and the joy in our life will be constrained. Difficult relationships will undermine our happiness if we don't deal with them.

You can use this exercise to learn if you can trust someone, or if you should date or marry someone, or want to learn how to overcome relationship problems with anyone.

Guided visualization exercise for answers about relationships:

In this visualization you will meditate and go to that wonderful place of relaxation you have established as your own private sanctuary. When you get there, take a few deep cleansing relaxing breaths.

- Look around and take in your surroundings. Listen to the soothing sounds of nature for a while.

- As you are relaxing you notice that something is coming toward you. When it gets close enough you see that it's a beautiful horse. The horse is very friendly and speaks to you. He tells you that someone is waiting to speak to you. He asks if you will be so kind as to get on his back and ride him. You tell him you will and get up, easily climbing on his back.

- He takes you through a beautiful forest along a path that runs along a creek. You can hear the water rushing over the rocks. It's very beautiful. You hear the sounds of a hawk cawing and circling overhead.

- After a while, the forest ends and you see the terrain change. It becomes very mountainous. The horse begins walking up the mountain, on a well-worn path to the mountain's summit. Finally, you

reach the peak. At the top you see a shimmer
It seems to glow and change color as the su
horse takes you inside and you slide off its
to a great hall.

- You enter the great hall and see a beautiful wom..
  front on a throne. You approach her; she offers you a sea.
  left. She introduces herself to you as the High Priestess of Relationships and shares that she is an expert in matters of the heart.
  You sit and she asks you to tell her what has been troubling you
  about your relationship. You tell her what has been going on and
  explain your concerns, needs, or desires in this situation.

- The priestess replies with words of wisdom regarding your inquiry and situation. After she has answered all your questions, you
  thank her. She tells you that she will be there anytime you have
  any further relationship matters to discuss with her. She wishes
  you well, and the horse carries you back the same way you came
  to your sanctuary.

- When you return to your sanctuary, thank the horse for leading
  you there.

Review what the priestess told you. Then take yourself out of this
meditation. Record what she said in your journal and act on her advice.

Checking in on your health

Nothing is better than feeling vibrant and alive. When we have our
health we have the energy to accomplish anything and to deal with any
challenges that might arise. When we are ill our energy is low and we feel
as though we can barely get through the day, let alone deal with problems. Your intuition can support your body to help it function at its best.

My intuition saved my health

Not long ago I had my first bone density test. The test results showed
I had early signs of osteopenia, a precursor of full-blown osteoporosis. I

shocked! How could this happen to me, I thought? I took vitamins and ate what I thought was a very healthy diet.

My doctor told me not to worry about it too much. She said I should step up my resistance exercise, take a calcium pill every day, and take the bone building medicine she was about to prescribe.

When I got to the pharmacy to fill my prescription something in me was resistant to filling the prescription. It just didn't feel right. I knew this was my intuition telling me to stop and listen. I was certain something else was going with my body that a bone building medication wouldn't help.

When I got home I began a huge Internet search for the things that could cause bone loss in women. After about a week of research, I felt that I knew what had been happening to my body.

A week later, I was in my regular physician's office insisting on a battery of tests. It turns out I was dangerously deficient in Vitamin D which, after researching the symptoms, I had been sure was part of my problem. I was given a prescription of 50,000 units of Vitamin D to be taken weekly for three months. I also had raised levels of a certain marker indicating I was gluten intolerant, just as I had suspected. Luckily, I didn't have a full-blown case of Celiac disease, which is an intolerance so severe that it can be fatal.

What had been happening to me was that in the course of eating what I thought was a very healthy diet packed with whole grains, my intestines had become so inflamed from the gluten that they weren't able to absorb the nutrition in the food I had been eating. I became Vitamin D deficient.

It took over a year for my Vitamin D levels to rise enough to go off the prescription. When I went back for another bone density test the next year, the bone loss had stopped. I was elated! It hadn't gotten better, but it hadn't gotten worse, either. I was able to save my health, mainly my bones, because I had paid attention to my intuition.

Visualization exercise to check in on your health

You can check in on your health and help your body heal by accessing the wisdom of your intuition.

Use your intuition to see if something is wrong with your body that might require medical attention. You should always seek a qualified physician if you are in pain or if you feel something is not right with your body. You can and should check in on your body every now and again to make sure everything is all right.

Say you have been experiencing some discomfort in your left ankle (Substitute any pain or discomfort you've been having). You don't remember injuring it but it's been aching a bit lately. **Try this exercise:**

- Go into your meditative state in the evening before you going to bed. Once you are relaxed, go to your sanctuary. Get comfortable. If your sanctuary is by the ocean, see the waves coming in toward the shore. Listen to the sound as they roll in and lap up against the beach. Hear the seagulls. Really try to see and feel whatever is appropriate for the place you call your sanctuary.

- Now imagine that you have your laptop computer with you. You open it. On the screen is an image of you. Your body is simulated on the screen in a three-dimensional image. You are not wearing any clothing. Don't feel uncomfortable. Send love to your miraculous body.

- You can maneuver the program so that the image rotates and you can get a close up of just your ankle in the spot where it hurts. When you have your ankle in view look it over very carefully. What do you see? Is anything different about it? Whatever you see there is right for you, even if you don't see anything different about your ankle.

- What are you feeling as you look at this image of your ankle? Did a memory of stepping off a curb at an odd angle the other day resurface? Do you just suddenly "know" that this is the beginning of arthritis? Allow your intuition to well up, and don't discount any image, thought, or feeling you get at this time. It's all relevant to your question.

Make sure you go to your doctor if any ache or pain persists. Self-healing is always a supplement to qualified medical help.

Give yourself a intuitive body scan

You can use this exercise to check in with your body just to make sure everything is all right. Of course, this is no substitute for a real doctor and, if you feel you need medical attention, you must get it immediately. You can give yourself a body scan from the comfort of your own bedroom using the body screening software on your "special" laptop in this exercise.

- Say you do go to the doctor with a certain complaint but nothing is found and the symptoms persist. You can go to your sanctuary, and pop open your laptop and see yourself up on the screen rotating.

- At some point you will become drawn to a certain area of the body. Press a button on your laptop to stop the rotation. You focus in on this area to see if it appears different in any way.

- Are there any unusual markings? Or does a symbol come to mind while looking at this part of your body? You may actually get a feeling about what might be wrong, too. Usually, when you do this exercise, you will have a sense of what might be wrong as soon as you hone in on this area of the body.

Trust what you get. Your first impression is usually right, then call your doctor.

Scanning someone other than yourself

You can use the previous exercise for yourself or to see what might be ailing someone you know. This is what medical intuitives do. If you are really interested in doing this, you might want to acquaint yourself with the anatomy of the body. Buy a book and study it. It will help you when you do medical intuitive work. I would recommend reading books by Caroline Myss, a very well-known medical intuitive, if you are truly interested in studying this.

Sending healing to our bodies

Try this exercise to help heal your body of any ailment or pain you might be experiencing. For example, say you pulled your back out when you were digging in the garden. You went to the doctor, but it still hurts. You can use this exercise to give you some additional relief from the pain.

- See yourself rotating up on the screen on your "special" laptop. When you see your back, press a key on the computer and stop the rotation. Zero in on the part of your back that is hurting.

- Activate the healing portion of the program and see a golden pink haze appearing over that part of your back on the screen. This is special healing energy created by the program just for your back. See it being absorbed into your back.

- Before coming out of your mediation say to yourself that this magical pink healing energy will work on your back while you sleep. Tell yourself that when you awaken in the morning, your back will be feeling much better.

When you get out of bed the next morning you realize your back isn't hurting like it was before you went to bed the night before. You are feeling great relief.

How to get the answers to life's problems

There are many ways to tap into your intuition. The basic way is to ask yourself questions and see how you feel, but sometimes we want more than that.

Here are a few more ways you can tap into your intuition to get solutions for the problems in your life.

Asking for answers and guidance

- Make yourself comfortable in a straight-backed chair like the one you meditate in. Go into a light meditation with your breathing.

Ask yourself the question you have been grappling with. Wait and see how you feel.

- If you still feel confused, ask the question again. If you don't get the answer at that point, tell yourself that you will get an answer within forty-eight hours.

- During this time period, each time you are meditating, reaffirm that the answer is coming to you. The answer will appear either through a person you speak to, or through something you hear, see on television, or read somewhere—or as an epiphany or aha moment in the next forty-eight hours.

It's very important that you have faith and believe this to be so. You must believe you are going to get the answer in order for it to show up in your life. The reason you need belief is that Greater Intelligence will never force the answer on you. Your permission is necessary to arrange things so that the answer is revealed to you. Your skepticism is registered as a negative, blocking your permission to arrange the circumstances for the answer to arise in your life in the specified timeframe. But, when you have faith and believe, that is registered as a yes for giving permission to move the players around on the chessboard of life so that you and the answer cross paths.

Asking for a direct sign

Use this simple method for getting yes or no answers:

- You can ask that, if the answer is "yes," that you find a penny or any loose change today.

- If the answer is "no," you will not come across any change on the ground today.

- You can also make it more difficult by saying that, if the answer is "yes," you will see a red rose today. (If you work for a florist or at a nursery the red rose is not going to work for you! Change it to something else, like a red balloon). Or decide that, if the answer is "yes," you will hear or read a certain word or phrase somewhere.

Visualization exercise for more complicated questions

(Download a free recording of this exercise at http://www.PoweredbyIntuition.com)
Go to the room where you meditate. Do your breathing and get into a meditative frame of mind.

- Ask the question you need the answer to. Now count backward from twenty-five to one. With each count see yourself walking down one stair on a flight of stairs. Each number takes you lower and into a deeper more relaxed state. When you reach one, you see a door straight ahead.

- You walk toward the door and open it. It's dark inside. You search for the light switch and turn it on. You see it is a store room and a sign on the wall reads, "Lost and Found." There are rows and rows of shelves with all kinds of trinkets, tools, and implements on them. You also see small figurines, a snow globe, binoculars, jewelry, clothing and even musical instruments. You notice piles of books and children's toys. Something catches your eye way in the back. You walk toward it, maneuvering between the shelves. As you approach you recognize it as _____. You pick it up and hold it in your hands. Is it smooth? Or is it cold or warm? Does it have any moving parts? Is it heavy?

- This object you are holding is the symbol for the answer to your question. Analyze this object: it holds the answer to the problem for which you seek a solution.

How did you do? Did you see the object? Did it give you the answer you were looking for?
I once did this exercise when I was considering whether or not to sell my home and "saw" an old-fashioned egg beater, like the one I inherited from my aunt. I realized I was tired of being "beaten" down by all the constant maintenance of keeping up a home. Then I remembered that

eggs symbolize new life and, by mixing them up with my egg beater, I could whip up a whole new life for myself where I was free of house payments! That helped me to make up my mind and, a few months later, I listed my house and sold it.

Meeting and working with your guide(s)

Each of us has a team of spirit entities, or guides, who are here to help us. You can connect to them and ask for their help directly. The experience is different for each of us. You may be aware of your guides and develop a deep relationship with them. Or you may only feel a "presence" or nothing at all. It isn't necessary that you meet your guide or work with your guide. If you receive information directly and don't feel called to work with your guides, there is no need to.

The benefit of a guide, however, is that it can help to focus on someone outside ourselves when we are trying to get the answers to life's problems. If I said, "Close your eyes and ask yourself what to do about this problem," you might freeze or your rational mind might take over and give you the wrong answer. However, if we are working with a wiser being, it may make us feel more relaxed about getting the answer. When we are relaxed, our intuition will come through much more easily.

There a few more reasons that working with guides can be very helpful. If you find you are stuck in your intuitive development, working with your guides can help you open up and expand your abilities to another level. It also gives us a point of focus. Rather than just asking for an answer and waiting, we become engaged in a dialogue with our guide where the answer can surface more organically. There is no better way to get spiritual guidance than working directly with your guide.

Follow these simple steps to connect with your guide:

- Relax in a quiet place and go to your inner place of relaxation: your sanctuary. Take a few relaxing breaths in through the nose and release the breath through the mouth. Still your mind.

- When you are in a meditative state speak to your guides. Silently tell them you want to meet them one at a time and that you are open to receiving their guidance.

- Silently ask that the guide you need to meet most at this time make itself known to you now.

- Imagine (see in the mind's eye) that you are walking up a gentle hill in the beautiful countryside. It's warm and sunny outside. You feel the warmth of the sun on your arms and face. As you reach the summit of the hill, you see a small figure in the distance coming toward you on the road. This is your guide.

- The guide raises an arm and waves to you. You wave back. The guide is still too far to tell whether it is a man or woman. Don't have any expectations. Your guide can take any form and be either sex, or even without a specific gender.

- You keep walking past trees and a small babbling brook. With each step the guide is getting closer and closer and more details are discernible.

- At some point you are able to tell if the person walking toward you is a male or female, although you can't make out his or her facial features yet. You see what your guide is wearing and can make out the colors of their clothing.

- Now you are face to face. You see your guide clearly. You both reach out and embrace. You have met a personality who cares deeply for you and whose only purpose is to safeguard your well-being. You feel the love emanating from your guide.

- Now the guide gives you his or her name. It is_____. Your guide's voice is gentle and loving.

- Your guide explains how he or she will help you and *may* even tell you what your purpose in life is. Don't be disappointed, if at the first meeting, all you get is an introduction. The guide communicates to you that they will guide you whenever needed. All you need to do is practice listening.

- Stay as long as you need to and then return to full awareness of your surroundings.

Don't forget to write down all the information you were given today. Remember, you can return to meet with your guide whenever you wish. You can also meet your other guides this way.

Make your first session introductory. Don't bombard your guide with questions at this time. Just listen. It takes practice and time to get accustomed to working with your guides, so don't try to go overboard the first time.

One word of caution, though: I would advise you to get used to working with one before you meet the others. The better you get at communicating with the first one, the easier it will be to hear the others and not get confused over who is "speaking."

You can check in with your guide(s) anytime you need guidance. The more often you work with your guides, the stronger your connection will become.

Some examples of spiritual topics you can expect help with from your guides:

Ask them for advice about your spiritual growth or whether you are on the right path spiritually, help to forgive someone, or how to open up your heart and become more loving and compassionate for example. Of course, you can ask your guides to help you with anything from finances to relationships and health, but they do delight in seeing you progress spiritually. Don't hesitate to avail yourself of guidance on their specialty!

Get answers from the wisest person you know

(Download a free recording of this exercise at http://www.PoweredbyIntuition.com)

Some of us are more comfortable with authority figures versus working with our guides. If you feel more drawn to get answers from an "authority," use the next exercise instead.

- Go to your meditation room and get yourself into a relaxed state. Do your breathing. When you are ready go to that place of inner relaxation you chose earlier. Visualize yourself at your peaceful sanctuary.

- Something catches your attention way out in the distant sky. At first it looks like a speck; then it gets closer and bigger. It looks like a pink dot and, as it gets closer, you see it is a large pink opaque bubble. There is a hazy figure of a person inside. The bubble slows down over your head. You are not afraid at all.

- The bubble lowers to ground level. A door opens and inside the wisest being on the planet awaits. Who is it? Do you know him or her? Is it a figure from history? This wise being may be your grandmother, a former teacher, the president of the United States, Albert Einstein, or even King Arthur.

- This wise being beckons you inside the bubble. You get up and step inside. The wise person tells you that he or she is aware of your problem and is here to help. You pour your heart out to this wise, loving soul. Afterward the wise being instructs you on exactly the steps you need to take to solve your problem or gives you the answer directly. The wise being says that he or she will assist you anytime, night or day. All you need to do is call his or her name and this wise being will come to your aid.

- You thank the wise being and exit the bubble. The door seals shut and the bubble takes flight up into the atmosphere. You are very grateful to have the answer and a friend with such wisdom.

How was it? Was your question answered? Were you surprised by who your wise being was?

Don't feel bad if your wise being didn't speak to you. You may "feel" the answers rather than hear them. Or at first you may need to "make up" the dialogue, but after a while your relationship will take on a life of its own. Try to practice meeting with your wise being once a week after this initial meeting. Call it "Lessons from My Wise Being." Think of one question to ask each week pertaining to your spiritual growth such as, "How can I be of help to the world?" It's good to do this on the same day at the same every time. This will make it more of a habit.

Many people have received very valid information this way. In fact, entire books have been written based on conversations with "wise beings." Have you heard of *Conversations with God*?[2] Neale Donald Walsh wrote an entire book based on a series of questions he asked this wise presence, which he felt was God. You are connected to this same Greater Intelligence and it is waiting to assist you.

Have you ever heard of *A Course in Miracles* channeled by Dr. Helen Schucman?[3] Or *Seth Speaks*, channeled by Jane Roberts?[4] Or the intelligence who calls itself, *Abraham Hicks*, channeled by Esther Hicks?[5] All these books were channeled from Greater Intelligence by their "authors." I put authors in quotes because they themselves will be the first to tell you that the book wasn't written by them; rather, it was given to them. They were only the mediums for this communication. So, don't discount this method of getting information. It can really work for you.

---

2   Walsch, Neale Donald, *Conversations with God: An Uncommon Dialogue*, (New York, Penguin Putnam, 1995).
3   Schucman, Helen, *A Course in Miracles*, (Temecula, Foundation for Inner Peace, 1976)
4   Roberts, Jane, *Seth Speaks*, (New York, New Awareness Network, 1994). Visit website for more information: http://sethlearningcenter.org/
5   Visit the Abraham-Hicks Foundation for books by Esther Hicks: http://www.abraham-hicks.com/lawofattractionsource/about_abraham.php

Chapter Six

Overcoming the Roadblocks to Intuition

"Never argue with a hunch."

—Florence Scovel Shinn

Why trusting only the rational mind will always lead you astray

The ego and the intellect are the two archenemies of your intuition. There is no room for logical thinking while you are working with your extrasensory perception. You can feel the difference between logic-based thinking and the intuitive process by asking this question: "Is this something I 'know' I must do, or am I feeling that I 'should' do it?" Feeling obligated or rationalizing why you should do something is not how your intuition communicates to you. When your intuition speaks to you, you feel motivated and inspired, not obligated.

Intuition is innate intelligence or primal knowledge; it just is. It has to be accepted by a non-judgmental mind in order to be accurate. It's not to be made sense of. Making sense of things is using the intellect or logical mind again. To use extrasensory perception is to get in touch with a higher level of intelligence. The ego wants to control; the rational mind wants to find all sorts of explanations and to understand everything. These two actually block your intuition. In order to work with intuition, you have to accept what comes to you without questioning it. Only after you receive the image, thought, or feeling should you analyze it using the rational mind to understand it better.

Trusting your intuition brings the "fabulousity factor" into your life

When you trust only the rational mind you will never have the "fabulousity factor" in your life. Having the "fabulousity factor" means that serendipity and synchronicity are constantly working in your life, producing wonderful coincidences that solve problems or bring answers you need.

By using only the logical brain you are cut off from Greater Intelligence, which willingly responds to your every request. You are also relying on the ego, which can be very petty, controlling, and fearful. The intuitive mind is giving and supportive. When you receive guidance from your intuition it feels good, totally right, expansive, and full of light. It gives you a feeling of buoyancy and being in the right place at the right time and that another door has opened to you. When we make decisions purely because they make sense without checking in with our intuition, many times we will have a nagging thought at the back of our minds that we choose to ignore. This can later come back to haunt us.

When you rely solely on rational thinking you may have "talked yourself into something" or decided upon something because it makes sense. And that can be fine and it does have its place. Logical thinking is an important aspect that we need to survive. However, the best way to make decisions is to use both your rational mind and your intuitive mind. This way you have the benefit of a backup check on all your decisions.

How to make a proper decision using both your intuition and logical mind

When you are deciding upon something that is an important decision in your life there are two factors to consider. Does it make sense to do this? In other words, will it benefit you in some way? And, how do I feel about doing it? The first part relies upon your rational thinking and the latter your intuition.

Let's say you have been thinking of selling your house. First you need to know why you are considering selling. Is it to downsize and reduce the time and money you put into maintaining it? Or is it to lower your monthly expenses? Once you know the reason and benefits of moving the next thing to do is to check in with your gut.

Perhaps you have come to a rational decision and feel that selling is the right thing to do but something in you still doesn't feel quite right.

Exercise to check in with your gut to get a sense of what is going on:

- Place your hand on your abdomen and ask yourself why you are having the feeling that this is "not right." Stop and listen for the response. It may come as another feeling, a knowing, a thought or a picture.

- Perhaps what you sense is that now is not the right time to sell.

- With your hand still on your abdomen you ask when would be the right time to sell. You get a sense that you should wait until after your sister's birthday. It seems odd but you don't question it. It's the first thing that came to mind.

- Then you check in one more time with your gut, asking how you feel about waiting until after your sister's birthday. You feel a strong sense of relief and assurance that this is the right time to put the house on the market.

The matter is settled and, more importantly, you feel settled about it.

A week later your mother is hospitalized and you spend the next two weeks at the hospital with her. The day she is released is your sister's birthday. The following day you call your realtor and tell her you are ready to list the house.

Had you listed the house sooner, you would have been exhausted by trying to visit your mother at the hospital while also keeping the house as neat as a pin. You might also have regretted the decision and been sorry you put your house up for sale.

Now suppose you had ignored this intuitive feeling? You would have sold your house, but it would have been considerably more stressful in the beginning when your mother was hospitalized.

Here's one more example:

Say you have been planning to take a road trip for about a year. You and your spouse are just about to leave and something starts nagging at you. Your spouse is anxious to get on the road to avoid the traffic getting out of the city. You say that you feel something is wrong and want to check in with your gut before you leave. You close your eyes and sense a "hunch." You ask your spouse if the dealership checked the spare tire at the last tune-up. Your spouse isn't sure, but says it's probably fine, so you decide to get in the car anyway. An hour later one of the rear tires blows out on the car, your spare tire is defective, and you have to be towed to a gas station where your trip is delayed for several hours.

You can use this technique for any important decisions you have to make, especially when you have a lingering nagging feeling that won't subside. Many decisions we grapple with could do with some fine tuning. You intuition is the fine tuning.

How to know if your life is moving in the right direction

How many of us have struggled to know whether we were heading in the right direction? For example, you are involved in something and putting in a lot of time and effort and you wonder if this is really what you are supposed to be doing. Should you be spending all your time painting? Or should you be out looking for a job? Is the painting going to pay off or are you just deluding yourself?

Say you have started your own business and things aren't going all that great. Nothing bad has happened and you are holding your own, but you are just not feeling really excited about the business. The business you created to get you out of the nine-to-five rat race is starting to feel a bit like the same rat race you left in the first place.

This is also another good time to check in with your gut. It's very important to ask your gut how you feel about something, rather than ask if you should be doing this or that. Your gut is best used to check feelings since that is the language it uses to communicate in the first place. The gut isn't your rational mind, so you can't approach it with logic or questions based on rational thinking. You have to speak the same lingo.

To know if you are on the right path, check how you are feeling

- How do you feel when you are painting (insert your own pursuit here)? Do the hours fly by? Do you feel at peace and joyful when you are painting? If yes, then proceed to the next part.

- Place your hand on your abdomen. Take a few deep cleansing breaths in through your nose and blow out through the mouth and then ask, "How would I feel about getting a job right now?" Wait.

- What is the sense you get? If the sense you get is strongly negative probe further. Sit with this feeling and speak to it. Ask it (the negative feeling) why it is here. Keep asking questions until you pin down the answer, but remember do not phrase any question as a yes or no. Keep them open ended so that you can dialogue with your intuition.

- If the sense that you get is an urgency to get a job, probe that further. You may discover that you feel a sense of guilt about not working, or that you are really starting to feel tired of spending your days alone and would like to work part-time so that you can be around other people.

- The point is that by checking in with your gut you can dialogue with your feelings and really discover what is going on inside.

You will know whether or not you are on the right path by the way you feel. When you are on the right path you have no opposing emotions that cause inner stress. You are in total alignment with your goals both emotionally, mentally, and physically. When you are out of alignment there is internal friction that causes us to feel stressed and depleted. You can't enjoy the path you are on if you are worried about money all the time. When we have needs that aren't being met and that clash with our desires, we will experience inner conflict.

When the road you are traveling is the right one you will feel energized and excited by what you are doing. There will be nothing else pulling you down, no other concerns or emotions that detract from the experience of feeling that you are moving in the right direction. To know if you are on the right path check in with your gut and see what you are feeling.

Troubleshooting the blocks to intuition

Hearing your intuition isn't often easy. Don't make it any harder than it has to be.

Trying to separate an intuitive flash from the din of thoughts echoing through the mind can be nearly impossible at times—like trying to scoop the salt out of seawater.

Read through the list of intuition blockers carefully and see where you might be creating blocks.

One of the biggest blocks, especially in the beginning of working with your intuition, is not trusting what comes to you. You have to remember that working with your intuition is not the same as how the thinking mind works. It's not logical and not linear. Ideas appear in the mind wholly formed and complete when you get information from Greater Intelligence.

You don't have to think about the process or the steps involved getting there. Have you heard about people who suddenly get the idea for a book? It comes to them all at once, and they know the entire story down to the characters and plot outline? Or you might have heard about famous composers who received entire orchestrations in one downloaded thought? That is how intuition works. When you get a feeling or an answer, understand that you are going to feel as if you are making it up, but you have got to go with it.

Everyone feels as if they are making it up at first. That is normal and natural, so don't let it throw you. Trust it and just spit it out! Write down what came to you and then act upon it. Remember, if you don't act upon this wisdom, you are going to shut off the flow. You only get as much as you need and, if you don't use the supply you are given, your supply will be cut to match what you have used.

Another stumbling block to intuition is letting the pipes get rusty. You have to keep practicing. Have you ever heard the joke, "What is the fastest way to Carnegie Hall?" The answer is: "Practice, practice, practice." It's the same with your intuition. You have got to keep practicing to keep your intuitive muscle in shape. You also have to understand that you are never finished. There is always something more you could learn. There are hundreds of sensing modalities that our bodies use to get information to us, and we have only scratched the surface of understanding how they work. Use the exercises I've given you in the book to keep your intuitive muscle in shape. You wouldn't want to lose it, would you?

One more common problem is that a lot of people only remember their intuitive flashes after an incident occurs, not when they receive the flash forewarning them of the event. What this tells me is that they aren't meditating on a daily basis. When you meditate your mind is clearer. When your mind is clear you are more able to retain information and to hear and retain those intuitive flashes when they rush through. Another benefit of meditating is that your mind becomes calmer and you don't have that crazy loose squirrel running around trapped in your head anymore. Your thoughts are calmer and slower. There is more time between thoughts, and they don't all rush in at once and consume you. When you reach this level of mental clarity by practicing meditation regularly, you will receive more and also retain those intuitive flashes of insight.

Differentiating between the voice of ego and that of intuition is extremely important. You have to get clear on the difference. The ego will trip you up every time unless you have practiced enough to form a solid basis of knowing the difference. All these problems always go back to not laying a solid foundation with the basics. Meditation will solve all these problems. Make sure you read the rest of this chapter on learning how to discern your intuitive voice from that of the old trickster, the ego, thoroughly and then practice. Use the practice exercises in the book to learn from your own experience—how to tell the difference between what intuitive insight is versus your ego.

When you are impatient or uptight about making a decision you are usually tense. When you are tense you shut off the natural flow of intuition. It's sort of like when you were little and you went to the doctor and they wanted to give you a shot in your rear end. If you squeezed really hard the needle hurt more because it was so much more difficult for it to pass through your clenched muscles; whereas, if you relaxed it really didn't hurt that much going in. The anticipation of the needle was probably scaring you more than the actual shot itself. You need to calm down and not be so tense about things. Calm and relaxed is always the answer. Take some deep cleansing breaths when you are tense over a decision before working with your intuition. Impatience doesn't help either. Things are going to happen the way they are supposed to happen, so learn to let go.

Why unplugging from materialism is so important to developing your intuition

One of the biggest roadblocks in developing intuition is focusing too much on money. When we are all about how to make money or make more money or how can you get money, you are out of balance. It's similar to being a workaholic, really. Our society has become all about money and nothing else.

Money is the byproduct of doing something we feel good about where we are giving something of ourselves through our work to the world. When we focus only on money and are willing to do almost anything, short of it being illegal, we are sending out energy in the wrong order. The Universe hears our request and responds to it exactly, meaning that some of the essential ingredients to living a truly fulfilling life are also missing from the request. We might get money, but we might not have a fulfilling career, one that we love. And we won't be doing meaningful work that gives us deep satisfaction and joy. In other words, our entire lives will be all about the money—period.

I can attest to this from my own experience. When I entered the financial sales force I was looking for work that I could do part-time to make a little money while I was in graduate school. Within a few years the enjoyment I had for the business began to fade. It had become a grind, just like any other job I had held. I was only doing it for the money. Had the financial sales business been my passion, I wouldn't have lost interest in it.

The reason this is a roadblock to developing intuition is that you cannot have a single-minded focus on money and also be willing to let go and allow the Universe to provide or "catch you." When you focus on getting money, you are back in the mindset of thinking you have to "get out there" and "sing for your supper" in order to "make things happen." You have a deep need to be in control, which works in opposition to allowing the Universe to choreograph things for you. You are actually blocking your flow.

An intuitive flash is a terrible thing to waste

How many times did you hear about something and think to yourself, "I knew that!" You realize you had an intuitive flash about something but it was so fleeting that you ignored it. This happens to all of us. Many times it is over small things that don't impact our lives. But, when it is a big thing that could have potentially helped in a situation, you might find that you want to kick yourself.

Intuitive flashes tend to come at times when we are engaged in something else. It is usually something completely different than what the flash of insight has to do with. For example, say your daughter calls from college with a problem and needs your advice. You have a short conversation and hope that you helped her with her problem. While in the shower you are thinking about how many chores you have yet to do that day and wondering how you will get them all done when a brief thought flits through your mind. Your consciousness barely registers it as you focus on it for a split second.

The next day you call your daughter to see how things worked out; she tells you that one of her friends advised her to do something that solved her problem. You suddenly "remember" the brief thought you had in the shower, which was the exact advice your daughter's friend gave her. "Why didn't I call her when I came out of the shower?" you think. You feel a bit ridiculous that your daughter's friend was able to advise her better than you were.

The only way to capture these intuitive flashes is by setting the intention to become aware of them through concentrated effort and practice. Setting the intention is very important. This alerts your consciousness to emphasize the intuitive flashes when they come through. It tells your mind you want more of them and that you want to remember them.

How to capture more intuitive flashes

The next step is twofold. The first step is to begin a regimen of meditation every day, and the second step is to learn to observe your thoughts.

- In your next meditation set the intention to capture more of your intuitive flashes. Say to yourself during meditation, *I want to be fully aware of my intuitive flashes and have them register in my mind so that I remember them and can take action on them.* Then add, *and I will register them from now on and remember them.*

- When you state your intentions clearly during meditation your mind will begin to act upon them immediately.

Meditation will also help you with learning to observe your thoughts. A regular practice of meditation helps you remain calm and centered throughout your day. When you are calm you are less likely to create emotional drama in your life and fly off on an emotional tangent. You are more able to observe your thoughts when they are less emotionally charged. Emotionally charged thoughts pull you off center and into the emotion where you are no longer able to observe them impersonally. You become embroiled in them and lose your objectivity and focus. You might also start worrying and getting completely stressed over things.

Learning to observe your thoughts involves becoming more mindful and present. No matter what you find yourself doing throughout your day, keep checking your thoughts to see that you are fully present and focused on what you are doing at that moment. If you find your thoughts wandering off into the past or into the future, you need to pull them back into the present.

One great way to do this is by having a certain signal, such as snapping your fingers a few times, or pulling on your right earlobe, or saying out loud to yourself, "Be here now!" You can also put a rubber band around your wrist and snap it each time you find yourself wandering off. I'm not a fan of the rubber band snapping since it tends to pinch, but I know other people who have used this successfully to break a habit.

The reason you need to be fully present is so that you will be conscious of these intuitive flashes when they touch down lightly in your awareness. The more you become calm and centered the more flashes you will remember and the more you will have.

Meet the intuition blockers

Aside from the logical mind coming in and trying to override your intuition, fear of being wrong is the second largest block.

Fear of being wrong

When we fear being wrong we consciously edit the intuitive data we receive and give a "safer" response that seems to fit rationally and logically, rather than present the information we actually received. Getting over the fear of being wrong is very freeing. It takes some getting used to, but it can be done. You have to approach intuition as play, not taking it so seriously. Then the fear of being wrong will diminish on its own.

For example, I recently read for a Caucasian woman who asked me about a family member. I immediately got an image of an Asian man. Had I feared being wrong I might have omitted that I was seeing a man of Asian descent. I was not afraid, however, so I described the person I was seeing and it turned out that the family member was of Asian descent.

The need to be right

Closely related to the fear of being wrong is the need to be right. If you need to be right all the time, you are going to find working with your intuition difficult. You may second guess yourself all the time and edit what comes to you to what you "think is right," as I might have done in the previous example. You will need to let go of this to be successful with your intuition. Let go, let go, and let go some more. Intuition thrives on letting go. Your intuition is like a wild card—free and flowing—and the need to be right all the time is the exact opposite of what intuition feels like. You will inhibit your ability to recognize this voice if you continue wanting to be right.

It's also important to practice in a safe environment around people with whom you are comfortable and who support you. You can be wrong around people you trust and they won't make you feel silly or stupid. Make sure you practice under these conditions, and the fear of being wrong will soon disappear.

Relinquish control

To be really open to hearing your intuition, work on the need to control others or offer unsolicited advice all the time. Focus on yourself, your own growth, and what you are doing to better your life. Too much time focused outside of yourself on others will disconnect you from your own intuition. Many times those individuals who focus disproportionately on advising others on how to lead their lives are doing so in an effort to keep from facing and dealing with their own problems.

Getting enough rest

Getting enough rest is vital for hearing the intuitive voice. Having a good night's sleep is important. If you don't get enough sleep, your brain won't function at its optimal level. Your body will want to conserve energy by diverting it away from extraneous functions so that your heart and lungs continue working properly. On the days when you are tired, you won't have an easy time focusing on accessing your intuition. When you want to check in with your intuition for big decisions, postpone them until you are well rested.

Over-thinking and over-analyzing

Having a highly rational mind and over-thinking will also inhibit your ability to hear your intuitive guidance. If you are "thinking about something," then that is not your intuition. Intuition just happens; it's not a sequential mental process like thinking is. When you think too much, you have no quiet space for the intuition to come through. Don't forget, intuition is more like a whisper. If there is constant chatter going on in your mind, you will find it very difficult to hear the whisper above the din of noise in your head. Rational thoughts are the exact opposite of intuitive flashes or hunches and come from very different places. Your mind cannot generate thoughts and allow the intuitive flashes through at the same time, so learning to quiet the mind and to stop thinking so much is vital.

Trying too hard

Another block to your intuition is trying too hard. This goes back to what I said earlier about allowing your work with intuition to be more like play. When you want it badly, you are really trying to control it too much; this will shut out your intuitive voice as well. So, stop trying so hard. Just allow it to happen. The only answer is to let go. You can't scrunch up your eyelids and "try." Trying too hard will not make your intuition come through. You have to realize you are not in control. The answer doesn't come from your ego; it is coming from Greater Intelligence. The less you try and the more you trust that it will come, the easier the answers that you seek will flow into your conscious awareness.

Negative people

Being around skeptical people or people who don't validate and support what you are doing will make it harder to hear your intuition. The attitudes of these people will affect you and bring you down. You may lose your enthusiasm about working with your intuition and start to feel very silly. Try to avoid negative people, or least talking about this work with people who are not on board with it, until you have gained a lot of experience and confidence working with your intuition.

Keep it to yourself

The next intuition killer is telling too many people about your new-found abilities when you are still quite new at it. Wait until you have gained more experience and have had some success first. Oftentimes our friends are happy and excited for us and ask us to help them solve a problem. If we can't do it for some reason—perhaps we are having an off day—we might be embarrassed and feel like a failure. This will undermine our fragile confidence. So, steer clear of telling people and demonstrating too early on in the learning process.

Comparing yourself to others

One more intuition killer is comparing your abilities to others. There is always going to be someone you think is more talented than you. Realize that everyone is on his or her own intuitive development path and relax about it. Plus, everyone develops in his or her own time. He or she may have been doing it much longer than you have. If you find that you are envious of someone else, switch it up. Change the envy to joy and appreciation for what this person is able to do and know that you too can get there with practice. Why not compliment the person instead? Who knows, you may become friends and he or she may be willing to mentor you with your intuitive growth.

Fearing bad news

Worry suppresses your intuition. When you are constantly worrying that every fearful thought you have is a premonition of disaster you will never hear the intuitive voice. You can't be afraid you are going to hear bad news either. You have to let go of these thoughts. Your mind will play tricks on you because it wants to be back in control. Remember working with intuition is letting go of control. That is the ego again; it doesn't like losing control.

Worrying

Intuition doesn't swirl around the mind like our thoughts do. Our thoughts swirl when we are worried. We can't stop the same thought from playing over and over like a broken record. Intuition comes in, lands, and then leaves us with an impression; that is very different from how our thinking mind works. Intuition has a sense of finality. We know "that we know," in our gut, which is very different from how our thoughts work. Worry comes from the ego, not intuition. Let go of worry if you want to hear your intuition clearly.

Busyness

Busyness is another intuition inhibitor. We all live such busy lives today. We stay up late trying to accomplish everything on our to-do list. It seems as if we never have time to just enjoy life. Overdoing it will suppress your intuition. Our lives become out of balance when we work too hard and give ourselves no down time. Busyness creates stress. When we are stressed our minds are constantly bombarded with thoughts. When your mind is on overload, your intuition will not get through.

Electronics

Slow down. Turn off the computer and the television. Shut off your cell phone, too. All these devices interfere with tranquility. They are noisy and distracting, not to mention that being around all the energy frequencies that these devices emit can also distort our own energy frequency, jamming up the signals from our intuition. Whenever possible use a landline instead of a cell phone.

Focus on joy

Get rid of any extra tasks you are doing that aren't that important. Streamline your day so that you have more time to be quiet and go within. You don't want to be so burned out that your mind is too overloaded to hear the voice of your intuition. Schedule time to play, have fun, and do things that bring you joy. The more joy you bring into your life, the more your intuition will reward you.

Clutter

The environment in which you are surrounded can also block your intuition. If you are in a cluttered space or it is not clean, you may find your thoughts constantly straying back to the chores of cleaning and organizing that you have procrastinated about doing. These thoughts will haunt you and undermine your work with your intuition.

There is a saying among practitioners of Feng Shui who study people's relationships to their environment: "If your feet hurt, clean out the basement." This saying is applicable in doing intuitive work, whether you have a basement or not! A cluttered environment will affect you both psychologically and psychically.

You need a clean and inviting space to work in. It should be quiet and peaceful. Make sure you address these issues before you begin practicing. Create an inviting and soothing space for yourself. Open the window or sit outside and allow the sounds in nature to help you connect to your intuition. Get outside frequently and sit or take walks in nature. Connecting to the natural world will help bolster your connection to your intuition.

Fear of ridicule

If you are reluctant to tell anyone about your abilities, you may unknowingly block the flow of your intuition. We can inhibit our intuition when our subconscious mind gets the message that this is something we don't feel comfortable with. The best thing for this is to join a psychic development group where you can be with like-minded people.

Feeling ill or uncomfortable

Being uncomfortable, in pain, or under the weather may also block your intuition. Wear comfortable clothes. Don't put anything on that is too tight or uncomfortable for you. If you are in pain or not feeling well, refrain from doing any intuitive work until you feel better.

Overeating

Don't have a heavy meal right before you plan to do intuitive work. Your body will divert a lot of its energy to digesting and you may find that you feel drowsy. Wait at least one hour after eating a lighter meal to work with your intuition.

Overcoming the childhood programming

If you grew up in a family with parents who discouraged you from taking any risk or making your own decisions, you may find it more difficult to hear your intuition. If you always second guess your decisions and opt for the "safer" or more "logical" path, you will need to do some inner work to overturn this habit.

When the answers won't come

Visualization to open up to receive answers:

- Sit back and relax. Go into a meditative state and then go to your sanctuary and take a few deep and relaxing breaths. Ask your question.

- If the answer doesn't appear, ask again and imagine yourself floating on a cloud. From your vantage point in the sky, you are able to look down and see a lonely stretch of highway out in the country.

- You notice a billboard in the distance. The cloud moves you toward the billboard. You can see there is something written on it but are still too far away to make out.

- As the cloud moves you gently closer, you begin to make out the words. What does it say? Finally you can read it. It is the answer you were looking for!

- Another thing to remember with intuition is that many times the answer can be found in your environment. The answer may come later that day as something we hear on the radio, see on television, read in the newspaper—even on a billboard.

- It might also come through a friend while in conversation. Greater Intelligence knows enough to put these things and people in your path where you will have an aha moment and recognize the answer, so let it. That is why we call it Greater Intelligence; it operates through everyone and everything, and it can orchestrate things for us that we can't do for ourselves.

- Get away for a while. Do something completely different. Read a book. Take a shower or nice relaxing bath. Call a friend and chat for a bit. Go visit a nice bookshop or run some errands. Just get your mind off your question for a while.

- Get out of the house and go for walk in nature. Hearing the wind swishing through the trees, birds chirping, or the sounds of the ocean will do wonders for naturally switching on your intuition again. When we are relaxed our intuition flows.

The single most important thing you need to remember

Developing intuition is very similar to getting in shape by exercising. You start an exercise regimen and do a different workout every day to work different muscle groups. After a few weeks, you find yourself back in shape. Your muscle tone has improved and your fat levels have decreased. You feel great. But, after some time passes, you begin to get lax with your exercising and eventually make excuses about being too busy.

Before you know it, you have stopped exercising. Your body slowly starts to lose that fit and toned look. A year later you decide to try again and you have to start all over again to get back in shape.

Your body will retain the cellular memory of being in shape and you can always get back on track. It's like riding a bicycle: once you learn you won't forget, although you will be a little rusty at the beginning.

Your intuition is very similar. If you don't work at it and keep it in shape, it will diminish as well. You need to find ways to incorporate it into your daily life. If you don't use it, you will lose it. You will also want the Universe to know that you still have the same level of intention so that all those marvelous coincidences continue to occur.

You don't have to be a professional psychic to keep your intuitive muscles in shape. The best way to keep up your intuition is to make it fun.

Twenty-five fun and easy ways to incorporate intuitive exercises into your daily life

You won't even know you are exercising!

1. **Create an intention to remember your dreams and record them.** Before going to bed, go over a problem you are having and, in your mind, ask for guidance. Be patient. It may take a few nights to either remember a dream, if you are not in the habit or to get the answer.

2. **Meditate.** Everyone says this. Why? Meditation helps quiet the mind. You want to slow down the mind chatter to expand the quiet spaces between thoughts. The longer the quiet is between thoughts, the more easily intuitive guidance can get through and be heard.

3. **Go for quiet walks in nature.** Quiet reflection in nature helps create the same quiet spaces between thoughts as meditation. Did you get an idea about the best way to deal with a situation in your life?

4. **Start guessing who is on the telephone.** Pause for a second before answering, and don't look at the caller identification or the phone number on the screen. Ask yourself who it is. See what pops into your mind.

5. **Try to envision what a friend will be wearing before you meet him or her.** Take a moment before leaving the house, or getting out of the car, to ask yourself what he or she is wearing. What comes to mind?

6. **Ask a friend to concentrate on one interesting object in their home; see if you can visualize it.** You can do this while on the phone with a friend or by picking a specific time when you are both concentrating on this task. Give your friend your impressions.

7. **Take a relaxing bath or shower and ask your intuition to give you the solution to a problem you have been pondering.** Let your mind wander. What ideas bubble up?

8. **Think of a challenge you are dealing with, then close your eyes and see yourself plucking a thick book off a shelf in a library.** Open it to any page. What is written on the page? Is it your answer?

9. **If you need a yes or no answer.** Tell yourself that, sometime in the next forty-eight hours, you will know the answer to be yes if you find a penny. Did you find a penny?

10. **When driving in your car with the radio playing see if you can guess the next song the DJ plays?**

11. **Tune in to your feelings when faced with decisions.** Notice if you are feeling excited, energized, or drawn toward doing one thing over another. Feelings of fear, dread, and procrastination are signals not to proceed with something.

12. **When at the grocery store or bank, stop for a moment and ask yourself which line will move fastest?** Then get on that line. Were you right?

13. **If you have a bird feeder, ask yourself which bird you will see first this morning at the feeder?**

14. **When meeting someone for the first time become aware of your "first impressions."** As you get to know them, determine if you were right.

15. **Try some inspired writing.** Go somewhere quiet and meditate for a short time. Then ask for guidance concerning a problem you are trying to sort out. Pick up a pen and start writing. Try not to "think" too much about what you are writing. You may feel funny at first but, after warming up, you may find yourself writing and writing. Was this the guidance you needed?

16. **Before you get to a busy intersection, try to see if you know if the light will be red or green.**

17. **Prior to meeting friends at a restaurant, test yourself to see if you know what your friends will order for dinner.**

18. **When going to the grocery store, busy coffee shop, or deli you frequent, ask yourself who you will see there today?** Who pops into your mind?

19. **Focus on any past successes with intuition.** Remember how it felt when it came through. Knowing how it works for you will enable you to identify it in the future.

20. **Ask a friend to concentrate on someone he or she knows and you don't know.** Try to see what impressions you pick up. Share with your friend. Did you see what they looked like? Did you get gut feelings about their personality or emotional state? Were you right?

21. **Take a deck of regular playing cards.** Turn them over face down. Hold one in your hand. Do you get an impression as to whether it is a black card or a red card? Take it further: what suit is it? What number is on the card? Did you have any hits?

22. **Before leaving your house, see if you get an impression about the traffic.** Are certain roads snarled? Has there been an accident? Is there a detour due to construction? Then turn on the traffic report to see how accurate you were.

23. **Is anyone you know having a baby?** See what your intuition says the sex of the baby will be. You may have to wait nine months to see if you are right!

24. **When going to someone's home for the first time, see if you get an impression about whether they have pets.** Are they dog people, cat lovers, both? No pets?

25. **Try this exercise with acquaintances. Have everyone exchange keys rings.** See if you get an impression about what their house looks like, the kind of car they drive, or anything else that comes to mind that is triggered by one of the keys. Do you see a safety deposit box? Their office building? A hand-carved antique box with love letters inside?

You don't have to use all of these

Just pick the ones that appeal to you. You may be quite amazed by your results. But, don't worry if you are wrong—only Carnac the Magnificent was right all the time! Fear and "stage fright" shut off your intuition. Remember that intuition is the opposite of rational thought. The two cannot occupy the mind at the same time. Intuition is spontaneous, playful, random, and operates independently of the intellect. Give some of these exercises a try and have fun. Once you get over the fear of being wrong, your intuition will soar and roar loud enough to be heard!

Are you beginning to "feel" the difference between thoughts that arise from the intellect and those that result from intuition? What are the differences? Take out a sheet of paper and note what you have learned so far.

Chapter Seven

Finding Your Passion, Purpose, and Authenticity

"Intuition becomes increasingly valuable
in the new information society precisely because there is so much data."

—John Naisbitt

Becoming fearless

When we gain enough confidence by using our intuition successfully we become fearless. We know that everything always works out. When we are fearless, we take more calculated risks and, in doing so, interact with more people and come across more opportunities. When we are open to more options the Universe has ample opportunity to orchestrate situations that match our blueprint.

If you sit at home all day, the only opportunity the Universe can line up for you is sending someone to your door with good news of some sort. That is a lot harder than being out in the world and coming in contact with many people in different places, where the Universe can send help and answers through a variety of channels.

The more confident you become by trusting that the Universe hears you and will respond to you the more fearless you will become. At the same time, the more fearless you become, the more opportunity you give the Universe to choreograph synchronous events in your life. Finding your passion and purpose requires that you become fearless.

How to discover your passion and purpose

Our intuition is one of the greatest tools we have to discover our passion and purpose in life. When we are aligned with our passion and purpose it is because we have heard and followed our intuitive guidance. Most people who are unhappy with their lives have never connected to their intuition. If they had, they would have known early on that they were embarking on the wrong career path.

In order to discover your passion and purpose, you have to be open to hearing your intuition. If you are open to your intuition, chances are you have already discovered the passion and purpose of your life. When you are linked into these two, your life will be sensational and extraordinary. You will be connected to an endless source of creativity and original ideas. The "fabulousity factor" will be part of your everyday life.

Serendipity or fortunate coincidences and synchronicity or meaningful coincidences will manifest to bring you to where you want to get to, only better! In other words, you might have a vision for your life once you embark on your purpose, Greater Intelligence will intercede and take you to places that are even more beneficial for what you are trying to accomplish—with gifts along the path that ramp up your success to astounding levels.

Your passion is your own personal pot of gold

When we find our own personal pot of gold we have found that thing that makes us tick. This is our passion. It is the source that feeds us and energizes us. We can't wait to wake up and start another day. When we are involved in it the hours fly by, but to us it feels as if it is been only a minute.

We are often told that we should be "living our passion," but many of us struggle to know exactly what that "passion" is. People stuck in jobs they hate always have the same question, "Why can't I find my true passion?" The answer is simple. Without first learning to hear the voice of your intuition, you will never truly connect to your passion. You will always listen to something outside of yourself and be disappointed.

Your intuition is a direct communication from your higher self. You are here on Earth for a very specific reason. It's not an accident. We are spiritual beings having a human experience for the purpose of learning and growing. Have you ever heard of the "school of life"? This is it. To tap into your intuition is to reconnect to your spirit, get help and guidance, in order to make this learning experience easier for you.

Are you a parent?

Have you ever advised your children only to have them reject your advice and choose to do things their way? Being a parent, you have gained experience and wisdom and know that this child is choosing to live life the "hard way" by ignoring your advice and guidance. This is the same with our higher selves.

When we are closed off to our intuition we don't hear this valuable advice

We are hell-bent on relying solely on logic to make decisions or driven by fear or what we think we "should do" and we end up feeling as if we are constantly pushing a boulder uphill. This is living life the "hard way."

Your intuition is there for a purpose

Follow the guidance of your higher self and allow the flow of life to easily get you where you want to go. This is the difference. Both methods may get you where you wish to go, but one way is hard and the other way is much easier.

Follow your intuition

Following your intuition is not about fortune telling—it's about developing an innate ability whose function is solely this; to help you live a more successful life.

- When you learn to hear the voice of your intuition, it will direct you to the right person at the right time—just when you need them.

- Your intuition will direct you to take one fork in the road over another and you will be led to something much more incredible than you ever would have if you had followed the "logical" fork in the road.

- Opportunities will arise that you never dreamed of simply because you are allowing something much greater than you to guide you and are in sync with the universal good that is there for you.

- When you are in sync, the Universe brings the world to you by positioning serendipitous and synchronous events on your path to help you utilize all the gifts and abilities you possess so that you may share them with the world.

Who would you rather have guiding your plane in for landing?

Is it someone on the ground who can only see the runway or someone way up in the control tower who can see if there are other planes circling that might pose a danger to your descent? I'll bet you said the person in the control tower, right?

When we connect to our intuition, we are receiving the benefit of wisdom from a much higher perspective. I don't know about you, but I'm pretty sure I don't know everything and I can't see everything that might be coming at me in my life. So, I would much rather allow the wisdom of my higher self to come through.

Following intuition is not for sissies

It takes guts—more guts than listening to logic. It is a leap of faith but one that will ultimately bolster your self-esteem and confidence like nothing else. The first time you jump from a plane, it's damn scary; after a few minutes, when the parachute opens and you realize you are not going to die, it is exhilarating! It's the same with your intuition.

After a few leaps of faith you "know that you know." There is nothing more exciting or exhilarating than the adventure of following where your intuition leads you.

Your passion is not hiding from you

More than likely it is right under your nose, but your logical mind has discounted it so often that you are no longer connected to it. Your passion is that pesky idea that you have had since you were a kid that never really went away. That thing you fantasized about doing when you were little. That subject you just couldn't read enough about and still tend to talk about. Reconnecting to your intuition will reconnect you to your passion.

I've always known what my passion was

One night I was having dinner with a friend. We were discussing where we would be in our lives if we had followed our hearts early on in our lives. I said without a moment's hesitation that I would be writing full-time instead of freelancing here and there in my spare time. I took a long detour through the business world and, while I learned a lot and appreciate all the opportunities I was given, I always knew that writing about metaphysics was my true calling.

She shook her head looking very forlorn. "Do you know how lucky you are?" she asked. "I have no idea what I want to do. I only know for sure what it is I don't want to do."

I realized she was right. I was lucky.

The million-dollar question

Then she asked, "How did you know that writing was it for you?"

I gave her a rundown of some things I remembered from my childhood that had pointed me in the direction of writing. It started her thinking and, by the end of the night, we had some ideas of what she might really like to do.

The conversation continued swirling around in my head on the way home. I knew there must have been more clues than I was able to share with my friend during dinner.

The next morning I journaled about this. Here is what I came up with:

How to unearth your passion with these clues

Answer the questions as you go through the following exercise.

1. **Look to what you loved and enjoyed doing as a child.** What were you fascinated by back then? Looking up at the stars? Reading? Collecting rocks? Grooming horses? Writing poetry? Could you do this for hours on end without noticing the time whizzing by? *I loved reading. I would take a flashlight to bed and read under the covers.*

2. **What came naturally to you in school?** What were you good at? Was there one subject you never needed to study for that you easily got good grades in? Was everyone always telling you how great you were at something? *I wrote and illustrated little books when I was a child.*

3. **What did you dream about doing when you grew up?** When you played, was there a theme to your games? Were you always the same character in the games? Did you have a secret fantasy you never told anyone? *I always fantasized about seeing my book in the window of a bookstore.*

4. **What was your favorite afterschool activity?** Did you play an instrument? Sing in the choir? Act in the school plays? Live for afterschool sport? *I loved going to the library and bringing home stacks of fresh books to read.*

5. **Is there an aha moment that stands out from your childhood?** Did you see a character in a movie and decide that was what you wanted to do? Did you read a book and find yourself dreaming about the life of that character? *I remember reading a book about the Bronte sisters and thinking, "That is what I want to do."*

6. **What do you enjoy doing in your spare time now, as an adult? Do you find that you easily spend money on this interest?** Reading? If so, what books do you gravitate toward most of the time? Playing sports? Which sports? Cooking? What type of cooking? Doing crafts? What kind of crafts? What are your hob-

bies? *Writing is still number one on my list.*

7. **Is there a topic of conversation you always find yourself bringing up?** Is it a topic you could discuss for hours? Have you studied it on your own and become an expert? Do you long to be with
the friends who share this interest? If you don't meet with them or
partake in this interest on a regular basis, do you miss it intensely?
*The topic I most love to discuss is using and developing intuition which
is why I write about it.*

I can't imagine anything worse than going through life not knowing
what it is you would love to do. Except maybe taking twenty or so years
to get back to doing what you love—but that is the subject of another
book.

**Think back to your childhood and see what comes to mind. Are
some of these clues there? Did you follow your passion or did you take
a long detour like me? Where are you now?**

Using visualization to help you identify your passion and purpose

You may need a half-hour or more to complete this visualization, so
be sure to set aside enough time.

- Go into meditation. When you feel completely relaxed imagine
that you are on a huge luxury yacht. Feel the wind on your face as
the vessel moves through the waters of the sea at a fast clip. The
captain brings you downstairs to a private theater below deck. He
seats you in a comfortable lounge chair and offers you a beverage.
See the room. It is luxuriously appointed with polished brass and
gleaming wood trim. In the front of the room is small stage that
has a curtain.

- The captain tells you he has prepared a special show for you. The
show is about you. You will be watching yourself at certain ages
when you were a child and enjoyed certain activities that hold the
key to what your passion and purpose is.

- He dims the lights and a spotlight illuminates the curtain. As the curtain goes up, you see the set is of your childhood bedroom. All the toys and books and furniture in the room are exactly as you remember. Then you walk out onto the stage as a child of ___ years old (you will recognize how old you are when you see yourself).

- Allow your creative mind to fill in the rest. How old are you? What are you wearing? What are you holding? And, most importantly, what are you doing? Watch as you play in your room. What did you love to do then? What interested you? What fascinated you? You are able to get the answers to these questions before the scene ends.

- The curtain goes down and the captain appears before the curtain. He tells you the next scene will be when you were a bit older and will show you how these interests you had as a small child developed. He walks away.

- The curtain goes up again and you are a few years older. You are now ____ years old. Your room has changed a bit. Perhaps it was redecorated as you got a bit older. You see yourself enter the room. You look exactly as you did at that age. How old are you? What are you doing? What are you reading or playing with? What topic or subject fascinated you? What books were stacked on the shelves in your room? Your younger self expresses your thoughts at that age out loud as a monologue. What did the younger you say? What were your dreams and aspirations at that time? You get the message before the scene ends.

- The curtain comes down and the captain appears again telling you that there is another scene coming next where you are older.

- The curtain goes up and you see that it is a classroom from when you were in junior high school. It is exactly as you remember. You see a teacher up in front and you realize he or she taught your favorite subject. What was it? What fascinated you about it so much? Now you see yourself walk into the room. You look exactly as you did at that time. You are very animated while speaking to the teacher about your project. What was the project?

- Allow your intuitive mind to fill in the rest of the scene. What does the teacher say to you? Does she give you any words of encouragement or point out a strength or ability you had? You easily see what it was that you were meant to do before the scene ends.

- The curtain comes down and the captain appears and says he has one more scene for you to watch. The curtain goes up again.

- On the stage is the interior of a movie theater. It is dark and a movie is playing on the screen. It is your favorite movie of all time. What film is it? Why did you connect to this movie so much? You are able to relate the film's theme to your life purpose or the lessons you are here to learn before the curtain comes down.

- Now the captain reappears and asks you if you understand what your passion is and what your purpose is. You explain to him all that you learned from watching the scenes that were presented.

- Think about all you experienced for a few minutes before opening your eyes. When you do open your eyes, write everything down in your journal. Add anything else that might have come to you. Do you understand your passion and purpose now?

- How do you feel? Is it exciting to reconnect with your childhood dreams and aspirations? Can you see whether you are using the strengths the teacher pointed out to you? If not, why? Do you see how your life is meant to be like the lead character in the film you just watched?

Now that you have reconnected to your passion and purpose, meditate on what you can do to bring your life into alignment with these newly remembered aspirations. Each day in your mediation ask for an answer or sign for what the next step should be to incorporate the passion into your life so that you can start living your purpose. Expound on the answers you received in meditation in your morning journaling session to come up with actionable steps.

Authenticity

Until we identify our authentic selves and live according to the way that is most supportive of our authentic self, we won't truly connect to our mission and purpose in this life. For example, I spent twenty-five years in a business career. Inside I knew I was much more of a free spirit. I longed to do something creative, work from home, and make my own hours. I also had a desire to be around artsy creative people where I could dress in funky clothes and boots rather than suits and heels.

Perhaps you currently live in an urban area, but inside the authentic you is more productive living in a quieter setting? In the following exercise you will discover the authentic you.

Revealing the authentic you

Only you can be you. There is no one else like you on the entire planet. Your authenticity comes from being totally you in every sense of the word. What feels right for you in your life is different from what feels right to other people. What makes you tick is different. The kind of house you feel comfortable living in, the type of topics you like discussing, the activities you are interested in doing, and the jobs you feel drawn to are all part of your authenticity.

When you move toward becoming more authentic in every facet of your life, you will also be moving toward finding what you are passionate about and unearthing your purpose as well. The three are intertwined and dependent upon one another. Once you begin working toward one you also naturally begin working toward the other two as well.

To be authentically you means that you have integrated your passions and purpose into your life and are living congruently; in other words, there is nothing you do in your life that is not in accordance with your passion and purpose. Everything you do moves you forward on your journey toward completing your mission. There are no parts of you that feel out of place or not right. You don't go to work doing a job you hate just to make money while professing that finding peace is central to your life. If you believe that you need total peace in order to live your ife, you will also find a job that helps you achieve that peace rather than undermine it.

To achieve a life that is in complete agreement with your mission takes time. It doesn't happen overnight. The thing to keep in mind is that, each day, you should be making small decisions and changes that move you in the direction of achieving this alignment. When new opportunities arise check in with your intuition to be sure that this new endeavor is in line with where you wish to go. If it detracts or distracts from your mission, you should consider not doing it. If it helps you on your mission, by all means go for it. Over time, these course corrections and changes will get you to where you are living a completely authentic life that is in agreement with your passions and purpose.

Exercise to meet the "you" that you were meant to be in the life you were meant to live

This exercise could take twenty minutes to a half-hour, so allow yourself enough time.

- Go into meditation and then go to your inner sanctuary. Take in the sights and sounds of this beautiful tranquil place you have created for yourself. As you are listening to the soothing sounds of nature, a beautiful hot air balloon lands gently on the ground nearby. There is a man standing inside the basket of the balloon wearing a butler's uniform. He beckons you over to the balloon.

- You walk over and climb in. He says that he has been instructed to take you on a tour to reveal your authentic self. You are very excited. The balloon rises higher and higher into the air. You look down over the side and you are not frightened at all. You see the landscape below where your place of relaxation is. It is getting smaller and smaller as the balloon rises.

- The balloon flies over beautiful green countryside and rolling hills. Then it begins to descend. Down below you see a wide landing pad. It is desolate with nothing around it. The balloon lands softly and the butler tells you it's time to get out. He asks you to follow him up a hill. As you walk along this path, you wonder what is on the other side of the hill. Is it a busy bustling city, a quiet peaceful suburb or farm country, or does it lead to an ocean or a lake? You continue to climb up hill.

- Just before you reach the crest the butler stops and tells you that when you look down from the top of the hill you will see the environment that suits your authentic self to a tee. You walk to the summit of the hill and look down and see _____. It is exactly the place you dream of living. Everything about it is perfect.

- The butler asks you to take his arm. As you take it, you are magically transported to the center of the location that is ideal for your authentic self. You look around, feeling very at home. It is perfect. It is the place you have dreamed of living your whole life.

- The butler instructs you further. He tells you that when you turn around you will see your perfect home. He asks you to close your eyes, count to three, and then turn around. You follow his instructions to the letter and, at the count of three, turn around. When you open your eyes you see your perfect home. It is the place that would suit your authentic self most perfectly.

- Is it a large home, an urban loft apartment building, a mobile home, a cottage, an old farmhouse in the countryside? You are amazed. The butler leads you inside. He takes you on a room-by-room tour, starting with the living room. As you go through the house he encourages you to open the closets and cupboards and look inside.

- Everything you see is exactly the way it should be. Each room reveals another clue about who the authentic you really is. The food in the refrigerator and pantry tells you a lot about who your authentic self is. The style of decorating, the furniture, the paint colors or wallpaper tell you more about this unique person. When you get to the bedroom, you look through the drawers and the closets to discover the kind of clothing that suits your authentic self best. He encourages you to try some on; after all, they belong to you, he says. You put on the clothes and they fit perfectly. You admire yourself in the full-length mirror.

- Afterward, he leads you to more of the rooms that reveal the profession that would suit you perfectly. The room contains all the clues to tell you what this perfect vocation is. You can clearly see by the implements and technology in the room what it is you are meant to do. You feel a tingle travel up your spine. It is perfect—what you were born to do.

- Next, he asks you to decide whether to go left or right in the hallway. At either end is a door. You decide which door to go through and you step through this door. As you go through the door, you enter a room of mirrors where you see yourself reflected to infinity. Suddenly the mirrors change and contain images. You realize you are watching a three-dimensional movie. It is your authentic self going through a perfect day. You watch yourself getting up in the morning, readying yourself for the day, and then doing whatever comes next in your authentic life. You get to see the people in your authentic self's life. Who are they? What are they like? What roles do they play? This continues until you have viewed one entire day in the life of your authentic self.

- You are amazed at the wonderful life your authentic self is leading. The day ends, and the butler escorts you back to your personal sanctuary, retracing the steps you took to get here. Stay in your sanctuary for a moment, going over the details of what has taken place. Was it what you expected? Did it exceed your expectations? Was your authentic self different than from what you thought? Write down every detail of your experience in your journal. These are the clues that will open the doors to the life you were meant to live.

Many people who do this exercise are surprised to find that they have a completely different life than they ever imagined but, upon review, they realize it really does suit them. Don't be surprised if, after this journey, all kinds of marvelous things start occurring out of the blue that bring you closer to living the life of your authentic self.

Remembering your mission

First, what is your mission? Your mission is the overarching plan for your life and comes with a blueprint of your life. Your blueprint holds the lessons you desire to learn in this life and the steps you will take to learn them.

We want to experience many different types of situations during our lifetime to learn how to cope with them. We want to hit brick walls once in a while, as well as face challenges, difficulties, and problems that help us grow and develop by teaching us the lessons we need to learn. Some of us need to learn how to deal with making a living and supporting ourselves, others need to learn how to have better relationships with people, and some need to learn how to love themselves and others unconditionally. The lessons each of us must learn are different, but the one thing we all have in common is a need to unearth this lesson plan. That is why we need to learn to hear our intuition. Our intuition is the "sign language" that the Universe uses to convey this important information to us.

Exercise for remembering your mission and seeing your blueprint

This exercise could take twenty minutes or longer, so leave yourself enough time.

- Go into meditation. When you are completely relaxed, envision seeing yourself sitting in your sanctuary.

- Next you see yourself walking toward a huge marble library. It is a huge building and very stately—almost like an ancient Greek temple. You walk up the stairs, past the beautifully sculptured pillars outside the library, and go inside.

- You are greeted warmly when you enter by a librarian wearing ancient Greek robes. She tells you that she is aware that you are here to look at your personal blueprint and leads you to a special room. She seats you at a table and pulls a long, rolled-up blueprint from one of the shelves. You notice you are alone in the room. She leaves you and closes the door so you can review the instructions for your life.

- When the door closes, you take the blueprint in your hands, open it up, and lay it flat on the library table. Speak to Greater Intelligence and ask that the purpose of your life be revealed and easily understood. What does it say? What is your purpose and mission in this life?

- Does the blueprint of your life tell you anything about why you have been floundering up to this point? Looking over your life as it is outlined on the blueprint, can you see why you needed to do the things you did up until now? How they might have prepared you for this mission? Does it explain the personality flaws you need to address and areas of your character that have been strengthened by all you have encountered? Can you see why you were born to the parents and family you have?

- Take as much time as you need. Once you have absorbed all that the blueprint has to tell you, put the blueprint back on the shelves and leave the room and go through the library.

- Stop by the librarian's desk and tell her you have finished. She will ask you if you now understand your mission. Tell her that you do and explain to her what it is. Don't be surprised if new insights surface during this conversation or if the librarian offers any more insight. Thank her afterward and leave the library.

- Come out of your meditation and record everything you learned in your journal.

How does it feel to know what your purpose is and to know what you are here to learn in the school of life? Are you on course? Do you need to make some changes in your life?

Drawing your map

How to get there:

Once you understand your purpose and the lessons you are here to learn, you can start drawing your map. Up until now you have been walking blindly on many different paths, some of which have been circles that kept taking you back over the same ground again and again. Armed with the knowledge you gained by looking at your blueprint, you can now draw the map of the path you need to follow to get where you are going.

Say you realize, after reading your blueprint, that you are here to learn to believe in yourself and your abilities and gifts. You see how your difficult early life of growing up with a single mother who worked long hours and left you in charge of caring for and feeding your two younger siblings was a blessing in disguise. As a result of these difficulties, you have an incredible talent for cooking, and your gift is that you love to feed people and make them feel at home and welcomed. You understand that teaching what you know about cooking is an important skill to pass on. You realize you have a desire to teach children—mainly at-risk kids who come from troubled homes—how to cook. You can see yourself doing this and you can feel how fulfilling it would be to help children develop a skill that will help them throughout their lives.

Exercise to create your mind map

(Download a free sample mind map and blank template: http://www.PoweredbyIntuition.com)

Allow twenty minutes or more to complete your mind map thoroughly.

- Take a sheet of paper and put down all your ideas about making this dream a reality. You are going to create a mind map.

- Start with one word or one phrase in the middle of the paper. In our example, the phrase is, "cooking with at-risk kids," as that is the central idea around which the mind map will be drawn.

- Now add any activity that comes to mind regarding what you need to do, steps you need to take, or people you might contact, down on paper. The next few words could be: give cooking lessons, create an afterschool program, write a cookbook for kids, get in touch with head of the PTA, visit local restaurants, talk to manager of the local culinary store, or join the local chamber of commerce. Initially all you want to do is get all the ideas that have been circling around in your head out onto the paper.

- The next step with your mind map is to circle all the words or phrases that feel like the right steps for getting the project off the ground and making it happen. Those steps (words/phrases) should be connected to the central idea in the middle with a line, so that, eventually, you have all the ideas that you want to pursue linked with a line to the central idea. Don't worry about being neat.

- Once you have the mind map drawn, you can take the steps and put them in order of what needs to take place when. After you have the steps in order, take each of the steps and put them at the top of a separate sheet of blank paper as you are sure to come up with smaller steps and activities that will be needed to arrive at each of the top headings on your page. Allow yourself to write these steps without worrying about their sequence. You can sort them out later.

- If you found the process of mind mapping the original headings helpful and enjoyable to your process then, rather than put the heading at the top of the page, place it in the center of the page and create a new mind map for each of the major steps you need to take. Either way, you will end up with a very detailed "map" of how you plan to arrive at your goal.

- Once all the steps are in place, create one central document and put it all together. Break down the process into manageable chunks. You may even wish to insert timeframes for each of the steps and give yourself a date for when the entire process will be completed. If you do this, you can insert each day's activity into a daily calendar, either electronically or in a day planner—whichever you prefer.

- The point of "drawing your map" is to chunk everything down into small manageable activities to avoid becoming overwhelmed with everything you have to do to arrive at your completion point—the point where you can start living your purpose. Smaller frequent activities feel less overwhelming and improve your chances of getting to the "finish line."

Now you have your map done. How does it feel? Are you excited at seeing the steps of your journey on paper? Does it make sense? Can you see how the logical flow of activities you have listed will help you to arrive at your destination?

Keep your map handy, and refer to it daily and weekly in order to schedule the time you need to complete the activities you have designated for that week. Do not reread the entire document each week. If you do, you may get overwhelmed or insecure and not follow through. Just follow each day's prescribed activities. If, after completing the map, you decide you have left out certain steps or need to remove steps, go ahead and make the changes. Don't be surprised if people who can be helpful to you just start showing up. Once you are in touch with your intuition and mission, the Universe will engineer everything perfectly so that whatever you need is at your disposal just when you need it.

It is not uncommon to make some changes and adjustments along the way, but don't scrap the entire thing and start over. You may think you are perfecting your map, but what is probably happening is that a sneaky form of procrastination is taking over. Don't strive for perfection, strive for done.

One more note of caution: don't share the map with anyone or talk about it too much, unless the person is someone who is your greatest advocate and cheerleader ALL the time. The last thing you need is for their criticism to knock you off your wobbly new legs. My suggestion is to keep the map to yourself entirely.

Doing extraordinary things

When we tap into our intuition and allow it to flow through us, we can and will accomplish extraordinary things. We feel our connection to this intelligent life force that motivates us and energizes us. Our connection is so strong that it almost seems as if it is carrying us through the process of our journey.

When we are buoyed by this force the support assists us in dealing with the challenges that come up during the process of moving toward our goal. Even when we bump up against obstacles, the solutions and people who can help us get around the problems seem to appear almost as if on cue. The process continues seamlessly despite the problems. People looking in on our process from the outside may believe we were born under a lucky star for the seemingly miraculous ways our plans always seem to work out, but the truth is that it really isn't miraculous at all. It is simply the way we were all meant to live our lives when we use the Intuition Principle.

The difference is in the approach each of us takes toward our lives. You are back in touch with the blueprint you came here with, so that everything you need is already there for you when you arrive at each step of your journey. Other people, who have not learned how to remember their blueprint, struggle with the problems of always being in the wrong place at the wrong time. They don't realize that this is the cause of their problems and frustration in life. Instead, they blame themselves and attribute it to all sorts of things—mainly that they are not smart or capable enough or that they are unworthy of success and happiness. This is a shame because each of us arrives here with all the tools and abilities necessary to accomplish our goals.

Free will versus fate

We are not shepherded on our paths like sheep but allowed to discover for ourselves that utilizing our gifts in loving service to the world brings us the joy we had been seeking our entire lives.

Returning with a blueprint, which is merely an outline of the lessons and highlights of our lives, doesn't negate free will. We have free will to live any sort of life we wish and to take any path in life we desire. All avenues are open to us, and everything we undertake in life is our choice. Some of us are more open to the whispers of our intuition from a young age and find our vocation early in life. Others struggle and listen later in life and find it then; others never find it. We can and do have free will over the trajectory of our lives at all times.

For those people who never find their blueprint or their purpose, life is not wasted. They will still leave this life having learned many lessons, although they may not be the ones they really needed to learn most. Straying off your purpose may result in a more challenging and problematic life, too. The meaningful coincidences that arise to assist us when we are connected to our intuition won't be there, and we may always feel that something is lacking or not quite right about our lives. Without connecting to our intuition, we will never be able to put our fingers on it, though, and it will always be source of dissatisfaction in our lives.

The point of "remembering" our blueprint is not to give up free will but to be more aligned with our purpose and lessons. When we "remember" the blueprint for our lives we become conscious of our mission and pursue it with passion and enthusiasm. Everything feels right within. We are now connected to our authenticity and "all the lights come on" because all the currents are making a connection. Our life fits us and suits us to a tee, and there is no discord between who we are on the inside and who we are on the outside.

We start to live "on purpose," and everything in our lives falls into place in accordance with the direction and lessons that are part of our blueprint. We are using the gifts and talents we were given and following the path that will best expose us to all the lessons we need to learn. We understand that we are here to learn from the experiences that living a physical life provides. For how else will we gain wisdom?

The path we have plotted is wide. We can deviate far from the main trail and still arrive at our destination, hitting all the major marks and learning all the lessons programmed into our blueprint. Our blueprint is a malleable, living, breathing document that allows for each personal choice we make. It has no rigid, specific instructions. Rather, it contains the schematics of our talents and abilities as well as the inclinations we will have and a list of themes we will need to deal with in order to become healed—or more rounded and whole.

The path is never as narrow as saying you are to be an attorney and to win this specific case against the Food and Drug Administration. The same qualities that it took to become an attorney in the previous example may lead you use those talents of persuasion to become a leading expert and advocate of sustainable farming. Likewise, it may lead you to become a fundraiser for a non-profit organization that helps organize urban community gardens. The point is there are many paths that will allow you to express your interests and the unique abilities that you possess.

Being on the "right" path is about utilizing your gifts and talents by using them for a purpose that contributes to society. Your mission can never be about anything else. For example, it is never about becoming a multi-billionaire solely for the purpose of being rich, but about how you can use your great wealth and power to make a difference—whether it is providing jobs for people or becoming a great philanthropist. Your highest purpose and mission is always about giving back in some way.

Our mission

A benefit of finding our true purpose is also that through this process we have learned to speak the language of our intuition and discovered life's instruction manual. When we learn to hear our intuition we also quell any fears that we are alone and unsupported by the Greater Intelligence that created us. When we are born our spirit inhabits our body and we perceive everyone as being separate from one another and from Greater Intelligence, our source. This is a powerful illusion created by living in a body in the physical dimension. When we come to understand that we truly are spiritual beings temporarily housed in this "suit of flesh" and feel at one with all life, we will find that guidance and support from Greater Intelligence flows even more readily.

When we are conscious of and in resonance with our blueprint we have awakened to our own evolution. We take our place as part of the segment of the population that is conscious of their role in helping humanity and our planet. We become aware that there is no separation between human beings, any life form, or our planet. We are all a part of the "one" fabric of life that has been woven together to create our conscious universe. Our awareness places us in the forefront of a new age where evolution is no longer a reaction by an organism to its environment, but a conscious choice to evolve emotionally, mentally, and spiritually in order to be a positive force in the world. The instructions and map for how to navigate this new age are imparted by our intuition with each step we take.

Intuition is not a magic pill

Challenges are important to our spiritual growth and evolution.

Without them we have little drive or motivation to accomplish anything. Encountering problems creates inner tension that is eliminated only by dealing with the sources of the tension head-on. The result of dealing with them is that we become stronger and wiser. We are here to gain experience and wisdom by learning to solve our problems, while still maintaining an attitude of love and compassion.

Finding our purpose and carrying out our mission doesn't mean we won't face challenges and difficult times in our lives at all. We will, however, be more equipped to deal with them when we are able to get guidance from Greater Intelligence through our intuition. We will also benefit from the synchronicity of meaningful coincidences when we are in touch with our intuition, so that even if we hit rough waters we are sure to be guided to safety and our highest good.

Chapter Eight

Putting It All Together to Shape a Meaningful and Fulfilling Life

"It is always with excitement that I wake up in the morning wondering what my Intuition will toss up to me, like gifts from the sea. I work with it and rely on it. It's my partner."

— Jonas Salk

Now that you have gone through the book, I hope you can see how helpful your intuition can be to you in everyday life. Your intuition is the source of your most original and inspiring ideas and solutions. Using it is practical. Remember, intuition is not about fortune telling but about using it as a reliable tool and road map that you can pull out whenever you need answers and guidance in your life.

Who better to advise you than your very own connection to Greater Intelligence? Who knows you better than the intelligence that created you? You may have surprised yourself with all the wisdom that came through in the intuitive exercises you used in this book. Most people are very surprised when they are first introduced to this form of guidance. They wish they had been taught to use it much earlier.

Can you imagine how much more joy you would have experienced had you known that this blueprint and map existed earlier in your life?

After going through the exercises, especially the ones to discover your mission, true purpose, and authentic self, how did you feel? Many people tell me afterward that they never felt calmer and more certain in their lives. The fears that they had about following their intuition and a map that only reveals itself before you just one step at a time have disappeared. It is as if a huge shift had taken place within them and all the blocks that had been holding them back cleared out. Many have the sense that a new life is beginning.

The key is to relax when you are on this journey. So many of us deviated so far away from the path we were meant to follow and created all sorts of obstacles and drama in our lives because we chose to ignore our intuition. When you relax and enjoy your life your intuitive guidance comes through loud and clear. When you choose to ignore it the stress and angst you create when you are out of alignment with your purpose muffles the voice of your intuition and you end up more lost and more distraught. You need to remember and know that, even if you can't see where the path is leading you according to this ethereal map, to keep listening to your intuition and you will get where you were meant to go.

Using your intuition is the most amazing journey you can ever take. Once you begin the journey the most exciting part is that it will never stop. You step into your destiny when you choose to partner with your intuition. This destiny will be directed by the guidance you receive from your intuition and will take you places you had never dreamed you would go before.

- *Allow your intuition to guide you to the things you are passionate about doing, and you will sense just how "expansive" and "larger than this life" you really are.*

- *You will begin to feel the power within you that is greater than you coming through and buoying you up to new heights.*

- *When you are living your purpose and expressing your authenticity, unbridled joy, and excitement will stream out of you.*

- *Keeping the channel to your intuition open ensures that you will always have an endless stream of brilliant ideas and insights flowing to you that will bring your dreams to you effortlessly.*

After working with your intuition for a while, the calming effect of knowing that you can access the answers you need to address any problem that comes up is so reassuring that you become fearless—not in a careless risk-taking manner but like a well-trained warrior. You go through life confidently, unafraid of what awaits you around the next corner. The world becomes your playground instead of the big bad world out there.

With time, most people also see changes in their attitudes about money and possessions as well. When you know that you have this unbreakable connection to a Greater Intelligence that can supply guidance anytime on any matter, you start to relax about acquiring money. You are not uptight about it. You know it is there for you. This doesn't mean that you make irresponsible decisions when it comes to money, but it does mean you don't clamor after it like you might have earlier in your life. Relying on your intuition has given you a stronger faith and inner knowing that you will always be supported financially. Once you release the fear of scarcity or lack, the funny thing is that abundance starts filling your life in every area. It seems counterintuitive but, by letting go, we actually find that everything we desire starts to come to us.

As you adjust to this newfound understanding about always being supported, you also begin to treasure the experiences of life more. You understand that the reason you sought after money was because you believed you had to have it first before you could have the enjoyment and fulfillment you desired from life. But now you realize that you had it all backward. You now know that you must first seek the experiences that bring you enjoyment and fulfillment and that the money needed to fund these desires will show up when you are aligned with your purpose by following intuitive guidance.

Aligning with your purpose through your intuition is the path to your greatness and your abundance. There are many examples throughout history of individuals who were led by their intuition, rather than conventional wisdom and rose to greatness. Two of my favorites are the late Steven Jobs, the founder of Apple Computers, Inc., and Thomas Edison, the inventor of the light bulb. Jobs dropped out of college to found his business, and Edison was considered "slow" and homeschooled. Both men profoundly changed the world.

In June of 2005 Steven Jobs gave a brilliant commencement address to the graduates at Stanford University. In the address Jobs attributes the direction his life took to his intuition. It is obvious from his statements, that he knows that some of the best decisions we ever make in our lives are not justifiable by logic and the dictates of society.

A few gems from Job's speech as he explains what happened in his life after he dropped out of college make it clear that he valued this intuitive inspiration:

> *And much of what I stumbled into by following my curiosity and intuition turned out to be priceless later on.*

> *You have to trust in something—your gut, destiny, life, karma, whatever—because believing that the dots will connect down the road will give you the confidence to follow your heart, even when it leads you off the well-worn path, and that will make all the difference*

> *Your time is limited; don't waste it living someone else's life. Don't be trapped by dogma, which is living the result of other people's thinking. Don't let the noise of other's opinion drown your own inner voice. And most important, have the courage to follow your heart and intuition. They somehow already know what you truly want to become. Everything else is secondary.* [1]

—Steven Jobs

Thomas Edison's inventions changed the world. He was famous for his persistence, thousands of experiments, and afternoon naps. [2] Edison believed in working his imagination to get solutions and mentions this in his diary. [3] While he did not practice meditation, he attributed his supe-

1   Steven Jobs, "Commencement Address to Graduating Class of Stanford University," June 12, 2005. http://news.stanford.edu/news/2005/june15/jobs-061505.html.

2   The Smithsonian National Museum of American History Online, "The Lemelson Center Presents... Edison Invents!" accessed July 25, 2011. http://invention.smithsonian.org/centerpieces/edison/000_story_02.asp

3   Rutgers University, "The Thomas Edison Papers—Diaries and Journals," accessed July 25, 2011. http://edison.rutgers.edu/NamesSearch/Sin-

rior powers of concentration to his deafness and the lack of noise distractions. He devised a way to wake himself up from his short naps when metal ball bearings slipped from his hands. The short duration of his naps kept him in a twilight state, that nether-world between wakefulness and sleep where intuitive flashes of inspiration and brilliance are found. Many ideas and flashes of brilliance could have come to him while in this twilight state. Edison invented not only the incandescent light bulb, but the phonograph, and the film projector to name just a few of his inventions that were among the 1,093 patents he held. His inventions were ahead of their time. Like most visionaries it took a while for society to catch up to his genius, but society's conventions didn't stop him. Edison had the courage of to follow through on his hunches and in so doing he went down in history as one of the greatest innovators of his time.

Aligning with your purpose puts you back on the path you were meant to follow in this life that will lead to your own greatness. When you return to the path that most utilizes your abilities and gifts and begin sharing them with the world, you have synced with the Universe.

When you are in sync, the Universe brings the world and your dreams to you by positioning serendipitous and synchronous events on your path, which assist you in successfully completing your mission.

To be in sync with the Universe is to be one with the flow of life, where you sail with the current toward your goals with the same ease as a gently moving river, and that is the beauty of the Intuition Principle and the beauty of living a fulfilling and meaningful life.

<u>Epilogue</u>

Healing ourselves and our planet

"To laugh often and much; to win the respect of intelligent people and the affection of children ... to leave the world a better place ... to know even one life has breathed easier because you have lived. This is to have succeeded."

— Ralph Waldo Emerson

Developing our intuition is the key to changing our world for the better

Intuition is critically important for us to follow at this time in our history. In the centuries during which we have moved further away from listening to our intuition, we have become a world out of balance in many respects; emotionally, culturally and environmentally. To return to balance we have to return to a way of being where we not only rely on reasoning but equally on intuition, as well.[4]

Only when we are closed off to our intuition and spirituality could we possibly have such disrespect and wreak such violence on our planet. The repercussions of being cut off from our intuition are oil spills in our oceans, holes in our ozone layer, warmer temperatures that melt glaciers, increasingly volatile weather, and dangerous nuclear plants that could wipe out our entire population, just to name a few of the challenges with which we are now faced. The disregard for our planet is mirrored in our culture by a weakening of civility, harshness, and thoughtlessness.

The only way to heal ourselves and our planet is to go within and reconnect with the source of our intuitive wisdom, which is also the source of our connection with life in all forms. When we reestablish that connection to our intuitive wisdom, we also reconnect to the whole of life and feel this life pulsing within us and connecting us to all living creatures and our planet. We become more compassionate and aware that when we hurt another living creature, including injuring Mother Earth, we all feel the pain and suffer along with her.

Healing ourselves by returning to our natural state of being in tune with our environment also reestablishes our connection to the natural rhythms of the living world. When we feel this unity and connection to the pulse of all life everywhere we cannot hurt our planet; we cannot hurt another creature or human being. This is the only way we are going to save ourselves and our planet from the destruction our greed and need for more, more, more has inflicted upon our home.

Healing ourselves by reconnecting to our bodies

Taking care of the vessel you have been given to carry you through this physical incarnation is very important to your mission. That vessel is your body, and it is here to serve you and to contain your consciousness and spirit while you have a physical incarnation. If the body breaks down in the middle of journey you may not be able to complete your mission. It is critical that you respect and lovingly maintain your body for the duration of your life. Loving ourselves and our body paves the way for loving others—and all living creatures and our planet.

To put your amazing body into perspective, think of it as an expen-

---

4   Redfield, James and Carol Adrienne, *The Celestine Prophecy: An Experiential Guide*, (New York, Warner Books, 1995)xi -xviii

sive and highly advanced piece of technology created by the highest and most advanced intelligence in the entire Universe. This vessel has the amazing ability to be able to repair itself and comes equipped to last for upward of 100 years if taken care of properly. Your body is equivalent to the space suits that astronauts put on when they come out of their space crafts and move about in space. The space suits are equipped to provide oxygen to the astronauts, keep their body temperature even and protect them from the harmful effects of zero gravity outside the space craft. Our bodies can do all that and more, such as communicate with us to get our attention for things such as needing water, nutrition or medical attention.

I like to think of my body as a sweet innocent being, much like a devoted servant, that is on this journey with me. Whatever I desire is my body's command. My body loves me and is here to serve me on my mission and I love it. We are here together as a team. I couldn't survive in the three-dimensional world without it. I treat it with great respect. I give it the rest it needs and feed it the best food possible in order to keep it running in tip top condition. It responds to my loving care by exuding great vitality and perfect health and I am grateful.

In order to deepen the relationship you have with your body, you need to learn how to tune in to hear what the body wants to tell you. Some of us injure our bodies by smoking, drinking alcohol to excess, or by taking drugs. Some of us put all kinds of junk food filled with additives and chemicals that lack any nutritional value or we don't give our bodies the proper amount of rest to recharge. When the body breaks down and starts to show signs of disease it needs us to tune in and follow its instructions to put it back on the road to repairing itself. It can even tell us which foods it requires if we let it. So, learning to communicate with your body is vital.

Check in with your body at least once per week to see if it is happy and satisfied with the care you have been giving it. By checking in once per week, you will also be able to tell whether there is anything developing you should get checked out by a doctor before it becomes a major problem. Your body will communicate to you using the language of intuition and through physical feelings and sensations.

Exercise to connect to your body

Follow these simple steps once a week to stay grounded and connected to your body

- When you meditate, speak to your body and ask it if it has anything it wants you to do for it today. Place your hands on your abdomen and tell it that it is safe to say anything it needs to. Now take a few deep breaths in and hold for a few seconds and then release. When you feel calm ask your body to relay any messages or information about your health, or what it might need from you at this time.

- Listen. Pay attention to any hunches or fleeting thoughts that might arise. It is usually the "notions" we have directly after asking the question that contain the answers from our body. For example, perhaps you ask this question and then realize you feel very thirsty. You get the fleeting impression of an idea that momentarily touched down in your mind and it was to drink more water. You understand that your body is telling you that it wants to be given more water.

- Or perhaps you suddenly see the image of a bright sun, and radiating light and warmth flash through your mind. You have been feeling very tired lately and seem to have one cold after another. The image inspires this thought: Perhaps I need more Vitamin D, the sunshine vitamin?

- Maybe an image of a salad comes to mind and you realize your body is telling you to feed it more green vegetables. Or perhaps your body needs more rest and asks you to go to bed earlier? It could be anything. By honoring and respecting your body, by listening directly to its needs, you will find that your body works even more efficiently to provide you with energy and vitality to accomplish whatever it is you set out to do. It responds to the love and care just as surely as a puppy does by wagging its tail. Energy and vitality is the way your body wags its tail.

Your body is an intelligent creature and will help you if you allow it to speak to you and tell you what it needs.

Healing our planet

Many people are experiencing economic hardship and feeling immobilized by fears about the future. It feels as if there is a vice tightening its grip and increasing the pressure on us to accept a new way of surviving. Are you feeling it also?

The global shakeup we are experiencing is a signal that we have entering a new age in our history. We are struggling and grasping and clawing for security as our once thriving economy and societal structures, such as the banking and healthcare industries, crumble beneath our feet on the heels of a new era that is slowly taking hold.

Western society is economically dependent on consumption of mass-produced goods. This economic model has been exported all over the world—much to the detriment of our planet. Conspicuous consumption has become a requirement for economies to thrive, yet it is unsustainable; this is why we are in crisis across the globe.

If it is going to be, it's up to me

As this new era begins to take hold, each of us is given opportunities to make the changes necessary to adapt. At first, the Universe knocks softly on each of our doors to deliver its message that says it is time to reject all this false conditioning that tells us materialism is the way to happiness.

If we don't open the door to the initial message and act upon it, the Universe ups the volume. The next communication will not be as gentle. It might start out as overdue notices on bills, then calls from collectors, and the next thing might be a notice of foreclosure from our bank and then homelessness. It could be a rumor about layoffs and, the next thing we know we are handed a pink slip and we no longer have health insurance. The message could come through a marriage in trouble where values no longer coincide, and suddenly one spouse calls it quits and the security we "banked" on is gone. If we overlook the first few cues that are meant to wake us up in order to survive early on, the Universe will keep sending messages more loudly and violently until we *do get it.*

What the Universe is trying to communicate is that to deal with the challenges we are facing and the world is facing we need to fearlessly heed our innate wisdom or intuition. It is time to reject the excuses rationalized by the ego and time to return to checking in with our innate wisdom or intuition when making decisions in our lives.

You might be asking yourself what does becoming intuitively inspired have to do with recessions, political upheaval or even environmental calamity? While we were all so outwardly focused on acquiring the goods we have all come to accept as necessities for happiness in our modern day lives, we became closed off to hearing the subtle voice of our inner wisdom, our intuition. Once the acquisition mind-set became the standard and cultural norm, fear of losing all that was acquired wasn't far behind. When you add fear into the mix, you raise the stakes for maintaining the status-quo despite the obvious consequences. For example:

Did we really and truly think that pumping fossil fuel out of the ocean floor was safe and risk-free? Or did we all know deep down where our intuition resides that our addiction to oil was a recipe for disaster?

Did we really and truly believe that nuclear energy was safe and non-threatening to our environment even after Chernobyl and Fukoshima? Or did we all know deep down where our intuition resides that it was just a matter of time before disaster would occur?

Did we really think that we could support an endless rise and spread in consumerism across the globe? Or did we all know deep down where our intuition resides that this was unsustainable and calamitous environmentally?

Did we really think that we could continue living on credit cards and borrowed money in order to feed our insatiable desire for things? Or did we all know deep down where our intuition resides that we had been living beyond our means and would someday have to repay all this debt?

Did we "haves" think we could drown out the cries of the "have-nots" with our iPods, iPhones, and iPads forever? Or did we know deep down where out intuition resides that when one hurts, we all hurt?

We must realign with our innate wisdom; our world and every innocent creature in it is depending on it.

Collectively, we have been ignoring our intuition and allowing materialism to slowly snuff it out. But, we can't allow it to go on much longer. We are a world out of balance. The Universe has lost patience with us not heeding her calls. And she has spoken violently with huge storm systems brought on by changing weather patterns due to global warming. What more does she have to do next to get our attention? We can no longer afford to live cut off from our innate wisdom. To save our planet and our species we need to unplug from the decadent babble of the matrix that keeps us fat and docile on a diet of superficiality, shopping, and distractions like television. We need to become intuitively inspired leaders in touch with our innate wisdom, not afraid to buck conformity and courageous enough to speak the truth and act on upon it.

In this era, individual thought leaders and grassroots movements will reshape our culture. Creativity used to solve problems such as global warming will become the new highly sought after currency, and those who put it to use will survive and flourish. We will accept that there is a voice of truth and wisdom and that it comes from within each of us. Empathic connection and compassion will surmount power as cultural values. Awareness of the importance of honoring Mother Earth and nature will grow. Creating work outside traditional avenues that makes a difference in people's lives and giving back will become more sought after than the "golden handcuffs" that corporations hand out.[5]

Will you heed the call to become a role model for intuitively inspired leadership? Do you hear it whispering:

You are already whole and complete in every way. You don't need to buy everything under the sun to feel good — like the advertisers say. You can cut way down on your consumption of consumer goods and fossil fuel and be much happier. You can create meaningful work and give back to society, and yes, you can be a force for change and good in the world.

Are you ready for the next age?

---

5   Redfield, James and Carol Adrienne, *The Celestine Prophecy: An Experiential Guide*, (New York, Warner Books, 1995) xi –xviii, 246, 247

The Age of Intuition

We are entering into the Intuition Age,[6] a new age in our evolution based on intuitively inspired creativity that comes from knowing one's purpose through intuitive guidance and the desire to contribute something of value to the world and humanity. As more and more people are stirred in this new age to look within for answers and guidance the dominant culture of treating the earth with disrespect will be slowly diluted and replaced by a culture of respect for the earth.

The theory that humanity is now leaving the age of technology and entering "the age of intuition," was introduced by author Penney Pierce. I had long felt, as we approached the year 2012, beginning with my own awareness in the early 1980s, that growing numbers of people were opening up to metaphysics and spirituality, and much more willing to accept that the "unseen realms" were as real as our own plane of reality. When I came across this information in 2010 about the coming new age, the name fit perfectly for what I had been observing and feeling for so long.

Right now, the amount of information being created doubles every four years. That is quite staggering. There is no way any one person can keep up with such volume and growth in information. The result is that we are seeing the harmful effects of stress on the rise. Everywhere you look people are thinking about how to "simplify" their lives. People want to live with less and slow down in order to find a quality of life worth living again. Suddenly people are awakening to the fact that having too much and constantly chasing after material possessions is not as fulfilling as living more simply. What they are really looking for is a reconnection to their inner peace and intuition. They crave a slower, more meaningful life to have time to spend with their loved ones. Their intuition is screaming loudly, "Stop! Take time to love the ones you are with today." And people are starting to hear this message and beginning to listen to their intuition.

When we live such busy lives dictated by so much technology and activities that keep us up until late into the night we lose our connection to the inner voice. It is this inner voice that will return our lives to sanity and return the earth to a state of harmony.

---

6   Penny Pierce.com, "Welcome," accessed July 25, 2011. http://www.penneypeirce.com/

The intuitive personality is an evolved personality

When you start living an intuitively inspired life your whole world view will change. You will become clear about why you are on the planet at this time and you will be aware of and live your passion.

You will know better than to ignore your intuitive hunches. You will follow them as you know that they will open doors for you. You will develop the uncanny ability to "know" when you should do something and when you should back off. You will heed your premonitions about future events.

You will be connected to your body and aware of your feelings about things. Your head and heart will work together so that, when you make a decision, you automatically check on how you are feeling about it.

You develop an empathic connection to all living beings. You can read the emotions and moods of those around you. You have a knack for knowing if someone is going through a rough patch and is down. You are a good judge of character and you go with your gut, especially when it comes to first impressions.

You are open to change and flexible about the course your life should take. You will allow your inspiration to lead you to the next big undertaking in your life. You are also in touch with your creativity, and the ideas for new projects are always flowing.

Things always have a way of working out for the best in your life. You take the plunge and commit to making your passions and purpose a reality, which changes your life dramatically. You come into your true power and really shine because you have tapped into the source of all joy and creativity.

By looking within you will find that the Universe "brings the world and life of your dreams to you" by delivering the right people, situations, solutions and opportunities to your doorstep at the right time.

This will be you when you live by The Intuition Principle and start living an intuitively inspired life!

Acknowledgements

I'm thankful to my parents for their open-mindedness during my formative pre-teen years. Had it not been for their Jesse Stearn books I found on our reading shelves, I might not have ended up on this path. Reading Stearn's personal account of delving into esoteric topics led me to study astrology, yoga, reincarnation, and meditation. My interest in meditation led me to discover Jose Silva and the Silva Mind Method and to Sahaja Yoga meditation. Both these practices were life changing. I highly recommend both methods of meditation. Meditation has proved to be the single most powerful habit I have cultivated in my life and I credit my thirty plus year practice of it for opening up my intuitive and psychic abilities.

I'm grateful to Shakti Gawain and her book, *Living in The Light: A Guide to Personal and Planetary Transformation* (New World Library, 1998). Only after reading Gawain's book did I begin to understand the power of intuition to guide us in our lives. James Redfield and Carol Adrienne's, *The Celestine Prophecy: An Experiential Guide* (Warner Books, 1995), not only helped me further refine my philosophy of The Intuition Principle, as life's instruction manual but, helped me to realize I was on the right track.

I'm also grateful to Tom Bird. I dreamed of being an author since I scribbled my first little book at age ten. Tom's seminar made this a reality. I would also like to acknowledge Joe Wilner for including me in his Great Life Philosophies project. Had I not contributed an article to this collaborative ebook, I wouldn't have realized that what I had written contained the outline for my entire manuscript.

About the Author

Angela Artemis, an intuition coach, is on a mission to teach readers around the world to "speak intuition" so that they unlock all the brilliant potential that resides within and start living the life of their dreams now—not later. Her popular website, Powered by Intuition is a rich source of information for readers wishing to learn how to use their intuition to create happy, successful and fulfilling lives.

Her passion for teaching the art of "speaking intuition" stems from having overcome the blocks she had to hearing the voice of her own intuition. And, from seeing how her life changed dramatically for the better afterward when she started relying upon it. She believes that many of life's problems could be averted if only we would listen to our intuition rather than allow fear to dictate our decisions.

Ms. Artemis has trained with numerous renowned mediums, studied under several spiritual and metaphysics teachers, received instruction from an Eastern guru, and been a meditation instructor. She began her training as an intuitive at age eleven when she started reading the Tarot.

Ms. Artemis is also a financial sales professional with a twenty-five-year background in private banking and real estate finance. Her ability to navigate a demanding finance career while developing spiritually and psychically have given her a reputation as a very grounded and practical intuitive and medium. She also offers private readings, coaching, and mentoring for clients from around the world via Skype.

As a special bonus, Ms. Artemis is offering free downloads of work sheet materials and guided visualization exercises created especially for readers to help them find their true path in life and start living the life they've been dreaming of.

Visit her website, www.PoweredbyIntuition.com, to download your free bonus material today.

Ms. Artemis may be contacted by e-mail at Angela.Artemis.Author@gmail.com.

Glossary

Alpha brain waves: brain wave pattern indicating relaxed state

Applied kinesiology: a method of diagnosing the body using muscle testing to get feedback.

Aura: an energy field which surrounds the body

Authentic self: true to one's own personality, spirit, or character

Blueprint: a master plan for your life containing pertinent details for leading you to complete your mission.

Brain plasticity: the ability of the brain to change

Channeling: a means of communicating with a conscious entity not in human form

Clairalience: to receive an impression of a taste psychically

Clairaudience: to receive an impression of hearing psychically

Claircognizance: a direct knowing of information without obvious means of acquiring it.

Clairgustance: to receive an impression of an odor psychically

Clairsentience: the ability to sense what others are feeling emotionally or physically

Clairvoyance: to receive impressions of visual information without the use of the physical eyes.

Collective unconscious: those inherited feelings, thoughts, and memories shared by all humanity.

Divine grace: special favor or assistance received from the divine

Divine Mind: God, the creator, collective unconscious, higher intelligence, Greater Intelligence

EEG machine: a machine that records brain waves

Ego: the part of the mind that is conscious, most immediately controls thought and behavior, and is most in touch with external reality.

Electroencephalogram: a reading of brain waves from an EEG machine

Extrasensory perception: awareness of information about events not gained through the ordinary senses — also called ESP

Fabulousity factor: a life that is outstanding comparatively speaking and graced with fortunate coincidences such as synchronicities and serendipity

Field consciousness: a continuous field of intelligence, expanding through space and time.

Greater Intelligence: referring to God or creator, higher intelligence, the universe, divine wisdom, an infinite source of wisdom and intelligence

Guides: ethereal beings assigned to help and guide us throughout our lives

Gut feeling: a hunch or feeling of nervousness, apprehension or butterflies in the solar plexus area

Hologram: a special kind of picture produced by a laser and that looks three-dimensional

Innate intelligence: the wisdom of our intuition which is innate to every human being

Intention: a focused desire for a specific purpose

Intuition: faculty of attaining by direct knowledge or cognition without evident rational thought and inference

Intuition Principle:. *The Intuition Principle is the concept that within you exists an innate technology, your intuition, capable of both guiding you to and attracting to you the life and happiness you've always dreamed of.*

Intuitive Flash: a solution or answer to a problem that comes suddenly like a flash of insight

Intuitive guidance dream: a dream that answers a question or solves a problem

** spired life**: being led toward your good in life by relying on one's nspiration and guidance

...in thinking: reliance upon the rational mind to the exclusion of intuition

Metaphysics: the study of what is beyond human sense perception and the physical world

Multidimensional being: a person who is aware of their true nature as a spiritual being and able to receive guidance from the spiritual dimension via their intuition and to therefore, rise above worldly conditions.

Muscle testing: using muscle responses to dialogue with the body

Neural pathways: neural pathways connect different parts of the brain allowing for the flow of information.

Organized system of intelligence: a system designed to support and propagate all life

Pendulum: a device to get answers from muscle responses similar to muscle testing

Precognitive dream: a dream that foretells of a future event

Premonition: knowledge about an event that is to happen in the future

Presentiment: an emotional agitation warning that something is about to happen but, without any specific knowledge of what the event will be.

Primal knowledge: instinct or a sense of just "knowing"

Psychic: A person who uses natural intuitive powers for divinatory purposes

Raisen d'etre: reason for living

Rational mind: a way of thinking that excludes intuition

Remote viewing: to see something that is a great distance away and cannot be seen with the physical eyes

Second brain: the area in the solar plexus that we feel butterflies and a gut feeling in

Serendipity: an instance of finding or receiving valuable things not sought after, an unexpected windfall, a fortunate coincidence

Signs: a signal coordinated by the Universe to show you are on the right path

Sixth sense: a power of perception beyond the five senses, developed intuition

Sway test: use of the body as a "pendulum" to dialogue and get answers through the body

Synchronicity & Synchronous events: a meaningful coincidence

True calling: our passion and divine calling or avocation

Universal Mind: God, the creator, collective unconscious, Divine Mind, higher intelligence, Greater Intelligence

Wise being: another name for a guide

Index

A

A Course in Miracles (see also Helen Schucman) 100

Anxiety 24, 73

Aura xv, 6, 48

B

Brain, The (alpha waves) 58, 59

C

Christ, Jesus 72

Civility 151

Clairalience 54

Clairaudience 52

Claircongnizance 53

Clairgustance 53

Clairsentience 52

Clairvoyance 53

Confidence xii, 23, 25, 26, 27, 28, 29, 34, 37, 78, 113, 123, 126, 148

Conversations with God (see also Neale Donald Walsh) 100

Creativity x, xi, 19, 23, 24, 31, 36, 40, 45, 124, 157, 158

F

Fabulousity Factor xv, 102, 124

Fear 15, 28, 33

Feelings 21, 22, 25, 43, 48, 49, 50, 29, 65, 52, 72, 78, 82, 84, 81, 104, 85, 105, 119, 152, 120, 158

Feng Shui 115

Focus xiii, 3, 19, 21, 23, 24, 43, 48, 81, 84, 92, 96, 108, 109, 110, 112

G

Genius 2, 7, 8, 9, xi, 19, 23, 26, 9, 40, 41, 43, 28, 51, 55, 41, 59, 147, 148, 86, 149
    definition of 2, 7, 19, 23, 40, 41, 149

Greater Intelligence x, 1, 4, 5

Greater Intelligence (Collective Unconscious) , x, xi, xii, 1, 5, 6, x, xii, xiv, 6, 7, 11, 26, 30, 43, 44, 45, 67, 68, 68, 70, 75, 102, 94, 100, 124, 106, 113, 117, 137, 143, 145, 147, 144

Gut Feelings (see also Psychic Abilities, Hunches) iii, 7, 24, 7, 25, 43, 46, 48, 49, 50, 51, 32, 63, 49, 78, 80, 83, 103, 104, 105, 106, 114, 148, 120, 158, 165

H

Harmony xiv, 157

Hicks, Esther 100

Hunches iii, xvi, 22, 24, 7, 25, 43, 46, 48, 49, 50, 51, 32, 56, 36, 63, 49, 78, 78, 101, 83, 103, 104, 105, 106, 80, 114, 120, 148, 158, 165

M

O

P

Lightning Source UK Ltd.
Milton Keynes UK
UKHW010630011020
370850UK00001B/81